T0105518

Pathways to God

*Experiencing the Energies of the Living God
in Your Everyday Life*

Dr. Robert Newton, J.D., N.D.

BALBOA.
PRESS

A DIVISION OF HAY HOUSE

Balboa Press books may be ordered through booksellers or by contacting:

Balboa Press
A Division of Hay House
1663 Liberty Drive
Bloomington, IN 47403
www.balboapress.com
1-(877) 407-4847

ISBN: 978-1-4525-4639-1 (sc)
ISBN: 978-1-4525-4646-9 (e)

Printed in the United States of America

Balboa Press rev. date: 03/08/2012

Contents

SECTION III
Diet, Nutrition and Health Practices

SECTION IV
Questions and Concepts Relating to God

Forward

Probably the most elusive search in the life of most people is to have proof that God exists. Certainly this is the case for me, for since the age of four this has been my main quest in life. While it is true that most of us have been taught that God exists, it has been my recurring experience that people yearn to have proof positive of such an existence. People may know intellectually that God exists, but rarely or never do they feel this presence of God. People are just told "to believe" in God. I heard these things many times myself but was never satisfied with these explanations.

While the author has never been able to answer the question as to who or what created God, he can and will provide substantial proof of God's existence and practical methods, means, and devices, through which God reveals itself to us. He writes of these things from direct, personal experiences. Therefore, this book is not written as a theoretical treatise but rather from an inner knowledge and understanding. It was not until very recently that the author began to realize how many ways in which he had in fact experienced the life force energies of God. Yet he has been teaching these concepts for at least five years to many people.

Because his teachers and God have so generously shared with him, the author feels compelled to share these concepts with you, the reader of this book. He has been in the process of preparation to write this book for the entire forty three years of his life. When the idea for this book appeared, the author was openly ready to immediately undertake the task of its creation. Although most of the material contained herein may be unfamiliar to many readers, it is necessary for you to have an explorative and open mind to new and different concepts that will be presented. If you do this, you will either truly encounter God for the first time in your life in an experiential manner, or if you already have experienced God, your encounters will be even more profound and meaningful.

KNOW THAT NOT ONLY IS MAN SEARCHING FOR GOD BUT GOD IS SEARCHING FOR MAN!. **This is more factually correct than you may realize!** For while God never forces us to establish contact or partake of Its presence, **if we will take one step toward God, God will take at least a hundred steps toward us!** These concepts are prevalent in many of the world's religions and in the Edgar Cayce Readings. Thus God is very liberally dispensed toward us in that **God will always more than "meet us halfway".** The techniques, practices, and devices discussed allow us to take that "one step" which is our direct "pathway to God", as it were!.

Not only did the readings of Edgar Cayce predict a time of possible great upheavals on many different levels on Earth during the 1990's, this has also been revealed to us in the prophecies of Nostradamus, the Hopi Indians, the Mayans, and the prophecies of the book of Revelations in The Bible. We have further indications of the potential for great changes to take place on the earth from the sciences of Astrology and Numerology. In light of the probable changes to come, a strong relationship with God will be imperative just to survive on the Earth!

This is true because the Earth transformations could include unstable weather patterns, natural disasters, business and governmental deterioration and restructuring, familial and relationship realignments and disintegrations and the restructuring of religion as we know it today. This leaves the things and institutions by which we create stability in our lives in a major state of chaos. This may well force many people to search for the real pillar of stability in their lives, GOD, THE PRESENCE THAT WILL ALWAYS "BE THERE" for us!

But even if this worst case scenario of changes does not occur, there is still an extreme crisis which most people are experiencing today in their relationships—especially regarding romantic involvements. Unfulfilling and broken romantic partnerships are at record levels. And, the author has experienced this many times himself. Like most people, he always found the fault and cause of romantic problems to be created by his partner. However, the author finally learned that such problems are created by himself and his lack of a primary relationship with God!

Relief here, then, is spelled G-O-D (guidance on demand), if we desire better romantic and personal relationships!

Such relief comes in at least two ways. First, by making God the number one priority in our lives, we have the most powerful, loving and fulfilling presence in the universe as an active part of ourselves—much more so than the most fantastic and incredible romantic relationship conceivable! Secondly, by creating this hierarchy of priorities, we do not have the need to have unrealistic expectations and desires of another human being—which was not created, nor is able to fulfill such desires anyway! This should be and is the province of God, and this is listed as such in "Science and Health With Key to the Scriptures", by Mary Baker Eddy, and in Hinduism and Yoga!

These same concepts are just as applicable to alcohol, drugs, food, and any other addictions which we might have. It should not surprise anyone as to the extent of addictions and relationship problems which plague society today. Neither our families, nor our educational system, nor government, nor Western religions have done even the most minimal job in actually teaching and showing people how to know God in a relevant, experiential way.

The results of asking people to "just believe and trust in God" have borne the fruits of boredom, depression, disappointment and emptiness. This has led people to suppress or mask these disenchanted feelings with alcohol, drugs, food and many other addictive behaviors.

It is becoming increasingly clear that if we are to survive as individuals and as a society, we muse embark on a radically different course or courses than that which we have followed in the past. The author accepts that as these alternative approaches to knowing God are presented, because they differ from the accepted norms, there will be a strong criticism and backlash from the defenders of the "status quo". This is natural and to be expected since people normally defend that with which they are familiar and comfortable—even when it no longer beneficially serves them! One of the greatest minds of this century, Albert Einstein, himself experienced and knew this when he said: "Great spirits have always encountered violent oppositions from mediocre minds,"

The author has no need or desire to judge whether he is a "great spirit" or not. However, the methods, means and devices to more fully experience God, which are presented in this book, could be considered great and beneficial to all mankind! Although the majority opinion may dislike and/or dismiss the concepts presented in this text, this does not necessarily invalidate them! Some people have even declared, as the result of their experiences and a study of history, that the "majority" will usually embrace inferior and/or mediocre models and ideas. A pioneer or pioneers must come along to "shake up" and challenge the accepted beliefs of the masses!

Since the author has been one of these "pioneers" in one way or another for most of his life, he trusts that he is well prepared for this undertaking. His hope an desire is that your, the reader, will also be inspired and impelled by the "pioneer spirit", so that you, too, can access the incredible "life force" energies and Love which God gives to all of us if we will only let God become an active and functional part of our lives. Especially those people who are affected by, or who are recovering from alcoholism or other severe addictions, the author' desire is that this book will "set you free" and reveal God to you in a most powerful way! Certainly, you have an incredibly strong desire to know God whether you know it or not. If you think the "highs" you have with alcohol and drugs were great experiences, you can actually get much "higher" and control these "highs" as you learn to contact and experience the "life force" energies emanating from God! This book was written for the purpose that you learn to EXPERIENCE THESE "HIGHER HIGHS". With patience and practice, most reader of this book will achieve these euphoric states of god consciousness. This then ELIMINATES the NEED FOR and use and consumption of ALCOHOL AND DRUGS.!

So let us begin our quest for God!

This was composed in 1991 and very slightly revised in 2011

Acknowledgments

The author must express my gratitude for those individuals who have helped to instill the "pioneer" spirit in him and who have prepared him to experience God more profoundly in his life. To my parents, Nadine Feldheim and Charles Marvin Newton, he thanks you for raising him with a wide scope of vision so that he has been able to receive such a diversity of information as has made this book possible. Also, he is indebted to William Woolsey and John Alfred Clark, my Sunday School teachers. Without the spiritual concepts you shared with the author, he would not have been able to write this book. He is also deeply indebted to Reba Lawler, who introduced him to Christian Science and who is an inspiration to him, since she radiates God in her everyday life as much as any person he knows.

The author is also very deeply indebted to his first wife, Charlette Ann Smith, a quiet yet great woman who taught him through example and exposed his then closed mind to the spiritual sciences. Also an invaluable teacher to the author was Robert (Chuck) Charles Schwartz, who although he was younger than the author, was able to impart not only great spiritual teachings but also share many profound encounters with God. Another of his "young teachers" was Tim Latimer, a great Tai Chi Chuan teacher. He imparted to the author a consistently profound way to experience the presence of God. Major Virgil Armstrong also helped lead the author into many "unknown" areas of the esoteric sciences unlike any other teacher.

The short time the author studied with Dr. Harley Swift Deer Reagan, was an invaluable exposure to the teachings of the Native Americans. And his friend, Robert Mueller, was instrumental in stretching the boundaries of his spiritual knowledge and concepts. Also to Dr. Paul Spin, the author is grateful for revealing to him the aspects of God which he never knew existed!

The author is also grateful for the knowledge imparted to him by Mary Baker Eddy, founder of Christian Science and writer of the most profound book on God of her century, *Science and Health with Key to the Scriptures.* The writings of Dr. Fred Bell, especially in his book, *The Death of Ignorance,* have been invaluable to the author in writing this book. The author has been further aided by Dr. J.J. Hurtak's book, *The Keys of Enoch.* Also, the author is indebted to the extensive psychic "readings" done by Edgar Cayce and the cataloging of this information by The Association for Research and Enlightenment. Further, the author am grateful for the extensive research and book of Bruce L. Cathie in *The Bridge to Infinity.*

The author also desires to express his gratitude to the visionary scientists John Keely, Nikolai Tesla, Wilheim Reich, Albert Einstein, and Dr. Robert Becker. Besides the fact that their contributions to science are nothing short of revolutionary, their gifts to furthering man's understanding of God are even more significant and are only now just beginning to be realized today! Finally the author wishes to express his deepest gratitude to the Ancient Hermetic Order of Asclepiads. Through the Asclepiads he has been introduced to even more ways in which to know God, and his spiritual wisdom and understanding have increased at a greatly accelerated rate.

The author's special thanks goes to Asclepiads, Dr. David DeLoera, Hierophant, Dr. Henry Smialek, Neokoros, and Dr. Eldon Taylor, Hiereus, for the emotional, mental, and spiritual support they have provided me. In particular, Dr. Taylor's subliminal tape, "Spiritual Healing", unleashed my divinity in such a way as to bring this book into fruition. Also, this books creation was enhanced by the help of James Raughton, at Fox Publishing, and by my good friend Patrice Michelle Rybicki. Lastly, but not least, I am grateful for the students from my classes and seminars who have also helped me immensely.

CHAPTER 1

God Is Usually Subtle

Does God exist?

This question has probably been asked and pondered more than any other question on the face of the Earth. And the reason it has so preoccupied man is that God *SEEMS* to be a most elusive presence. In fact, most of the great religions have described God as "the unknown". "Seems" is emphasized however, because the author has realized after a very exhaustive search that God is not so elusive when you learn to become more "sensitive" so that you can DETECT SUBTLE WAYS by which GOD MANIFESTS IT'S ENERGIES. Although God is not usually "obvious" or "forceful", there are a few exceptions to this statement and we will discuss them in later chapters in this book.

Related to this question, although this is not apparent, is the question; "If God does exist, why do we experience emptiness, loneliness, sadness, and boredom"? The answer is that WE HAVE SEPARATED OURSELVES FROM GOD, and as we learn to develop our sensitivities, we can detect and experience God's presence which begins to dispel the problems listed above. This "sensitivity" is unleashed by learning to *RELAX*—a forgotten art in the Western world! But especially in the Eastern religions, the "secret" of relaxation has been known for thousands of years. Swami Satchidananda, an Indian master, has put forth the concept that when INDIVIDUALS LEARN TO RELAX, THEY BEGIN TO EXPERIENCE GOD'S PRESENCE more often in their lives, and the Universe is unfolded to them. This has also been put forth by Rajneesh (Osho) in his books and teachings.

This concept of relaxation is so obvious and direct, and yet the author has never encountered this idea in either Western religion or philosophy, except in the psychological works of Carl Jung. And, while it is not my intention to discredit or eliminate Western religions, their failure to emphasize relaxation has limited their practical effectiveness in our everyday lives. The BUSINESS, FAMILIAL, ROMANTIC, and SOCIETAL STRESSES which we all face today MAKE US VERY TENSE AND NOT RELAXED and thus WE FEEL AND KNOW GOD INFREQUENTLY, IF EVER! So we are left feeling stranded here on Earth by God, feeling generally inadequate or as dismal failures because God's presence continues to elude us, even in church!

Modern scientific research, as well as the ancient religious traditions, has begun to amass proof of the existence of God and of what God is comprised, during the several decades or so. This proof comes not only from physics but also quantum physics, quantum mechanics, and quantum and mechanical arithmetic. What we now know, as scientific fact, is that ALL THINGS, whether they be organic or inorganic, and whether they be liquid, solid, or gas, ARE COMPRISED OF ELECTROMAGNETIC ENERGY.

This, then, is as true of a rock as it is for man. We also know that this electromagnetic energy (or etheric energy) is comprised of light (including fire and color), vibration, sound (including music), and motion, as well as electricity and magnetism. All of this is the result of the operation of the atomic field and this is discussed in depth in Dr. Newton's book, *A Map to Healing and Your Essential Divinity,* in Chapter One and Chapter Five.

These subtle aspects—electro-magnetism, light vibration, sound and motion—of the "unknown God", are ways which allow us to profoundly know and feel the presence of the "known God", and by these we literally know our Creator! These energies of God, also known as the Life Force Energies, Prana, Pranic force, Chi, among others, are also the building blocks of Einstein's Unified Field Theory. This is discussed in depth in an Article by Ben Iverson in the journal of *Sympathetic Vibratory Physics* and by Bruce Cathie in his book, *The Bridge to Infinity*.

As preposterous as the proposition that God's essence is electromagnetic energy may seem to most people, we do know with certainty, from the thirty years of research by Dr. Robert Becker, that HUMAN BEINGS are at least, largely COMPRISED OF ELECTROMAGNETISM! Dr. Becker's findings are revealed in his book, *The Body Electric*. He has shown through extensive experiments that this can be established beyond a reasonable doubt in a biological sense in regard to biological life forms, whether man or animal!

Einstein apparently knew of this concept also since he described all PHYSICAL MATTER AS A "FORCEFIELD. We might well infer from this that Einstein was referring to an electromagnetic energy, since dense matter is incapable of producing a field of energy. Bruce Cathie relates to us in his book that the spectroscope shows there are intense electromagnetic fields around the Sun, and such energy is also responsible for every creation on Earth. Cathie has also brought to our attention that we now know the protons and electrons of our ATOMS are nothing more than CONDENSED "WAVE FORMS" and NOT PHYSICAL MATTER. These "wave-forms", of course, would most logically emanate from a central source of energy—GOD. There is a substantial discussion of how these atoms operate in Chapter One of Dr. Newton's, *A Map to Healing and Your Essential Divinity* and the parameters within which life and creation exists.

A depiction of God as electromagnetic energy will, no doubt, disorient and confuse those people who have felt that God is circumscribed within some type of body image with a long flowing beard and hair. But the question which must be asked is, have you ever really seen God in an anthropomorphic form as just described? Quite honestly, the author has never seen this nor does he know anyone who has, nor has he ever heard of this occurring. Yet he knows he has experienced God as electromagnetism, light, vibration, sound, and motion, many times in his life already and knows of many other people who have done so, likewise!

We also have God presenting itself to people in the Bible and other religious texts as fire and as light. The fact that God is comprised of these "subtle" electromagnetic energies, does not preclude that fact that God is also love, intelligence, etc.

As the author's studies with Egyptologist Chuck Schwartz have shown him, the Egyptians were well versed in the use of these "subtle energies". This can be derived from The Papyrus texts and inferred from the hieroglyphs and other Hermetic teachings. Also in China, the students of Taoism have known of these energies for thousands of years through such disciplines as the martial arts and especially Tai Chi, as have the Indians through Tantric and other Yogic disciplines. Such energies were also apparently known by the early students of the Kabbalah (Qabalah), and the early Native American Indian tribes.

We know from Genesis, in the Bible, that God created light. That the essence of God is "light" was proclaimed by the great mathematician and philosopher, Pythagoras. This we also know from *The Wisdom of the Ages,* by Manly P. Hall. We further know that God created/ manifested through the use of words, which invoke vibration, sound, and motions. These same concepts are repeated in the ancient Sanskrit (Hindu) teachings and other ancient religions. Plato, over two thousand years ago, discussed the substance (or real nature) behind the apparently physical appearance of creation. These concepts can be inferred also from the Egyptian hieroglyphs and Hermetic knowledge, which predated the Grecian religious and philosophic disciplines.

There are also indications that the powerful Greek healers, Asclepius and Appolonius, manifested their miraculous healings by allowing the etheric (electromagnetic) energies of God to pass through themselves as conduits to "charge" their patients. This use of etheric energies can also be inferred from Jesus' healings, since he repeatedly emphasized the importance of Spirit (which is essentially ethers or electromagnetism) over the "flesh" (physical matter). The fact that Jesus had such an intense halo around him shows that he knew much of this "special energy". It appears unlikely that any of the aforementioned people had electrometers, spectroscopes, Kirilian photography, EEG (electroencephalogram), or EKG (electrocardiogram) to measure the things that they "sensed" and utilized in their lives!

Over a century ago, Mary Baker Eddy, one of the most devout students of the Bible to this day, talked about the spiritual nature of God and the spiritual man created in the "image and likeness of God". This "spiritual nature" referred to in her book, *Science and Health with Key to the Scriptures, is* again the electromagnetic force field or "wave-forms" of energy we have already discussed. Today, however, through Kirilian photography, we have empirical evidence of the electromagnetic nature of man and objects (also known as the "halo effect"). We can also measure the electrical wave properties of our hearts with an EKG and of our brains with EEG.

If man was created in the "image and likeness of God", as the Earth's great religions have proclaimed, God likewise must be comprised of electromagnetism, since that is our basic essence—not dense matter. The ways in which these energies of God are manifested in creation is well documented in *The Death of Ignorance,* by Dr. Frederick Bell, *Stalking the Wild Pendulum,* by Itzhak Bentov, *The Bridge to Infinity,* by Bruce Cathie, and *The Keys of Enoch,* by Dr. J.J. Hurtak.

It would appear then, that we live in an energy universe created by an energy God. Gopi Krishna, in his book, *Kundalini for the New Age,* strongly puts forth the proposition, that after he searched the world's great religions, he realized that THERE IS MORE ENERGY THAN WE CAN EVER PERCIEVE, CONCEIVE OR USE! And he states, as the author does also, that such abundant energy is proof of God's existence and energy is a manner in which God "communicates" with us! Also, the Universe and the Earth have been fashioned on discernible mathematical patterns extending from the atomic level to the geographic level to the expanses of Space.

Many of these have been revealed in Bruce Cathie's book, *The Bridge to Infinity,* and in various issues of *The Journal of Sympathetic Vibratory Physics.* Does not such mathematical precision which exists on the Earth and the Universe, suggest an overriding energy and intelligence such as we would term "GOD"? Faith and belief, alone, will never completely open the doorway to atonement with God. However, if we have "understanding", as is expressed in the Gospel of Thomas, in relation to Jesus the Christ (this also would equal other "masters" serving God such as Buddha, Mohammed, Krishna, Zoraster and Quetzocoatl), God will truly be known to us—not just as a "convenient theory" but as a profoundly experienced energy and presence!

Refer to Dr. Newton's, "A Map to Healing and Your Essential Divinity . . . ." For further proof which profoundly indicates the existence of our Creator, God, where it is discussed how life exists within such limited parameters of energy that there must be some force controlling such!

let us examine specific methods which will give us this "understanding" and the relaxation that unlocks the power and presence of God, the chapters that follow!

CHAPTER 2

Mental Methods To Experience God

By using our mental processes, we have a powerful means by which we can experience the presence of God. It is true that God is omnipresent as was declared by Mary Baker Eddy in *Science and Health with Key to the Scriptures.* The problem is that while God is in fact ever present and always accessible to us, we "tune out" our consciousness to God by a variety of methods and by many different things that happen to us during the day. This "TUNE OUT" occurs as we become burdened by our jobs, families, etc., and we become EMOTIONALY UPSET—stressed, fearful, or angry.

One of the oldest, if not the oldest way in which we "tune in" to God is through prayer and meditation. Although many people feel that prayer and meditation are quite different, in fact they are directly interrelated to each other. As Edgar Cayce brought through in his readings, prayer is an aid in meditation as it causes us to focus on and strive for higher ideals. The elements that make prayer and meditation possible are a *desire* to contact God, *a focused intent* (which involves mental concentration), and a state of complete *relaxation.*

Furthermore, in prayer it is more beneficial to approach God with the intent of humbleness and asking for our will to be brought in alignment with the will of God. This is well described in the first chapter of *Science and Health with Key to the Scriptures*. Also in this same book, Mary Baker Eddy also reminds us that since God is omniscient (all knowing), IT IS NOT NECESSARY TO ASK GOD FOR YOUR NEEDS AND DESIRES SINCE GOD ALREADY KNOWS THESE THINGS.

Thus when we pray, GOD PRESENCE WILL BE MORE RELIABLY INVOKED BY EXPRESSING GRATITUDE FOR WHAT HAS ALREADY BEEN PROVIDED for us by our Creator as well as asking that we follow the will of God. God's presence will also be invoked through following the concepts emphasized in the Edgar Cayce readings of striving to become one with our Creator and to merge with the consciousness of God.

The element of RELAXATION IS THE MOST CRUCIAL ELEMENT FOR PRAYER AND MEDITATION for two reasons. First, a relaxed bodily state allows the electro-magnetic energy, as well as the other waveform aspects of God's energy, to powerfully penetrate and affect our entire body, thus making us more at one with God. Secondly, relaxation allows us to feel God's presence in our bodies usually as a warm and/or tingling and/or chills and/or vibration or sound in the head, hands, heart, or spinal column. Relaxation can be most quickly and effectively achieved through DIAPHRMATIC BREATHING, which is discussed in depth in the chapter on breathing mechanics and techniques.

In MEDITATION, rather than focusing on praising God, we are STRIVING TO ALLOW GOD TO COMPLETELY PENETRATE EVERY CELL OF OUR BODIES (actually this happens naturally but we tend to block this "process of penetration").This is achieved through a straight spinal column created by either sitting erect on the ground or in a chair or laying down flat on the ground or on a bed, face up. As has been known in the Eastern traditions of Yoga, Tanta and Taoism, these postures allow the electromagnetic energy of god to powerfully travel down the spinal column and be distributed throughout the entire body, Done in conjunction with deep diaphragmatic breathing, and visualizing a column of white, or gold or purple light penetrating the crown of our head, these are "INVITATIONS" THAT GOD UNDERSTANDS and by which God responds to us. The diaphragmatic breathing allows us to relax and it is this relaxation that allows us to more fully feel God's presence. The colors listed have been known for thousands of years as associated with God and deep spirituality. Color is discussed in depth in the chapter on color therapy.

The more we can empty our mind of its concerns of survival personal relationships, upsets and disappointments, the more room there is for God to penetrate not only our mind but also every cell in our body, which is facilitated even more when we are relaxed. When we are correctly connected and aligned with God, we will receive definite signals of feedback such as warmth and tingling in our hands and possibly even our bodies. We may also receive messages from God and those "master teachers" and angels aligned with God. These messages can involve guidance for us, solutions to problems or areas of our personality which need refining.

Bagwhan Shree Rajneesh, who now goes by" Osho", and who has had many deep meditational experiences, recently said that when we meditate that we become one with "light". In the author's many diverse meditations, he has felt this aspect of "light" manifestation, including radiating light, like a light bulb. He has also felt warm and tingling in his hands, head and spinal regions. This occurs because the entire body and brain/consciousness are "enlivened"/ "illuminated" with the "life force" /electromagnetic energy of God, as has been related in many of the Edgar Cayce readings. Cayce also brought forth information that MEDITATION ALLOWS THE AWAKENING OF "CHRIST CONSCIOUSNESS" in our lives. Also this will facilitate the process of eliminating subconscious "blockages" in the mind that prevent us from fully experiencing the Christ and God in our daily experiences.

Proper Meditation Procedure For Lotus & cross legged chair, & Back Prone .Lotus" & cross legged meditation position. This position is easier seated on a pillow or meditation pillow.

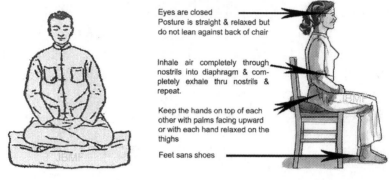

Eyes are closed
Posture is straight & relaxed but do not lean against back of chair

Inhale air completely through nostrils into diaphragm & completely exhale thru nostrils & repeat.

Keep the hands on top of each other with palms facing upward or with each hand relaxed on the thighs

Feet sans shoes

Lotus or Cross Legged Meditation

The Chair Meditation

Inhale completely into the Diaphragm thru the nostrils & exhale in the same manner & cyclically repeat.

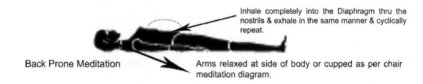

Back Prone Meditation

Arms relaxed at side of body or cupped as per chair meditation diagram.

It is very easy to go to sleep in this meditation position, so it is not recommended for most meditation situations.

Related to prayer, affirmations are positive statements about God and/ or ourselves, which put us in an optimal mental and spiritual state of functioning to allow us to more fully access God's energies and presence. As was discussed with prayer, whenever you praise God, God will respond in kind but with a higher response than you uttered with your "affirmation"! The author suspects this phenomena exists because God is such a prolific creator, especially if our recent astronomical examinations of the skies are correct! And this great abundance of celestial creation likewise extends the concept of our personal prosperity wherein it is believed by some "great minds" that God has a surplus of abundance for us far beyond that which the Creator could possibly bestow upon us. This does not mean that God is withholding things from us but rather that there is more abundance available than we could ever possibly need in our lives!

Very powerful affirmations about God and ourselves have been published in *Choose Once Again: Selections from 'A Course in Miracles'*; *Scientific Healing Affirmations,* by Paramahansa Yogananda; *Treat Yourself to Life,* by Charles Barker; various "Psalms" from *The Bible,* especially the "Twenty Third Psalm; the chapter of "Recapitulation" from *Science and Health with Key to the Scriptures,* by Mary Baker Eddy; and *Simple Things and Simple Thoughts,* by Dr. Eldon Taylor.

Affirmations, when done with your mental facilities, are repeated sub-vocally within your mind. For some people, however, affirmations seem to have more meaning and power when repeated vocally. If you have any doubt that the purely mental repetition of affirmations is effective for you, it would be advisable to use the vocal mode of repetition. This will discussed in more depth in the next chapter.

Affirmations about God and/or the divinity of man, benefit us in two ways. First, AFFIRMATIONS LET THE CREATOR KNOW THAT WE ARE DESIROUS OF ATTUNING TO THE PRESENCE OF GOD. Secondly, affirmations, if done every day for at least thirty days, WILL DISPLACE MISPERCEPTIONS ABOUT GOD WHICH MOST OF US HAVE IN OUR MIND'S. And they will REPROGRAM OUR MIND WITH BENEFICIAL AND

CORRECT PERCEPTIONS ABOUT GOD. These misperceptions alluded to, such as God does not love or care about me or need me as an expression of creation, cannot be seen by the eye and are oftentimes difficult to discover. Nevertheless, they are very real and destructive wedges which establish themselves between God and our selves. Also refer to Chapter Four of Dr. Newton's book, *A Map to Healing and Your Essential Divinity,* for a "Theta Consciousness Healing" protocol which can eliminate conscious and subconscious mental patterns that block the unleashing of God Consciousness in our lives!

Research undertaken by Dr. Eldon Taylor and other people who have researched the brain and consciousness, have shown us how tenaciously the human mind will hold onto a misperception, even something from the precognitive stage of childhood. This is also well documented in, *Imprints: The Lifelong effects of the Birth experience,* by Arthur Janov. Furthermore, there are a growing number of people, especially among hypnotherapists, who believe that we bring misperceptions about God and ourselves from previous lifetimes. This was often discussed in the Cayce readings, and also that it is imperative to replace all negative thoughts with positive thoughts. In Dr. Newton's *A Map to Healing and Your Essential Divinity,* this is discussed with more depth.

The more an affirmation is repeated, the more it exudes it beneficial effect in our lives and the quicker it will dissolve the "wedges and blockages" we have created between our Creator and ourselves. A simple affirmation that the author has used is: "I am a direct conduit of love, light and divinity, and I radiate these qualities of God to myself and others in all my pursuits. My only goal is to glorify and align myself with the will of God."

You may wish to create your own affirmation. You might relate to it more fully than an affirmation created by someone else! Concentrate on keeping everything contained therein, POSITIVE, UPLILFTING AND RESPECTFUL OF GOD. More on this related topic will be discussed in a later chapter on subliminal tapes and reprogramming.

Dreams and lucid daydreaming are other mental means by which we can encounter God more profoundly in our lives. For instance, if you ask for an encounter or meeting with God or another exalted spiritual teacher, to take place during your dreams, just before you go to sleep, this will often occur during your state of "dreamland". This phenomenon is revealed in many places in *The Bible* and other religious texts of our World, where God directed people to take action or solved problems for them while they were sleeping. Also, there are many instances in these books of people having "visions" from god, which could have in fact been dreams or lucid daydreams.

In lucid daydreaming, you allow yourself to drift into a completely relaxed state of being but instead of going to sleep, you remain awake. With your power of visualization, you can see yourself encountering the presence of God, and then with intense concentration, see and feel this event occurring. Many times, just this simple procedure will create a "meeting" with God. If you have trouble visualizing or want to do this more effectively, you will be greatly aided by, *Creative Visualizations,* by Shakti Gawain.

EXERCISE

Follow the procedure outlined earlier, involving the mechanics of meditating or daydreaming, and visualize one of the three lights with which you feel most comfortable, either gold or white or violet light streaming down into your head. While relaxing, fill yourself with the "life force" energies of God with one of the three lights listed above. See yourself climbing to the top of a very high mountain such as one of the Himalayan mountains or Mt Mc Kinley. And as is oft to happen in high mountains, clouds start to drift in and surround the mountain top.

As you look at the clouds, you see one with a chair in it which descends and you decide to sit down in it. As you do this, the chair begins to ascend upward into the skies above. The chair continues to accelerate at a rapid pace, and you are soon surrounded by many celestial objects. You begin to approach a blinding source of light. You continue forward and enter the light and as you come to the center of this mass of light, you stop and notice that the light is not blinding from this center perspective. In fact, you see combinations of colors such as would make the Aurora Borealis pale in significance. You feel this light and color penetrating every cell of your body, but most especially in your head, hands heart and spinal column. Allow yourself to become so immersed in this phenomenon of light, that you lose all concept of time.

Stay as long as you desire in this presence of light and note what is going on in your body—if any processes or changes are occurring. Also be aware of any mental feelings or messages. When you wish to come back to the World, summon your cloud and it will return you home.

Review any experiences during your meditation/daydream and reflect upon any messages from God or other enlightened masters which you may have received.

Now, let us examine vocal methods that invoke the power and presence of God in the next chapter

CHAPTER 3

Vocal Methods Which Affirm Your At-One-Ment With God

As was discussed in chapter two, many people prefer to repeat affirmations in a vocal manner. Usually when an affirmation is repeated aloud, it is called a mantra. A mantra, however, can be not only an affirmation; it can also be special words from a sacred language such as Sanskrit or ancient Hebrew, such as Aramaic. Mantras, for the most part, are alien to the modern Western mind. Although they are used in the Catholic Church such as in the Rosary, they often sound strange to us when they are formed from an unfamiliar language.

Mantras can be powerful because of the message contained therein and because of the "sacred sounds" from the sacred languages just mentioned or the activating vibrations of speech from any language. Through these vibrations—some more so than others—God can affect us with its life force energies; this has been revealed in the Cayce readings and is discussed in detail in *The Keys of Enoch,* by Dr. J.J. Hurtak. This subject of vibrations will be covered in more in depth in the chapter on toning, singing, and related concepts.

The power of these vibration energies from God are also discussed by Kirpal Singh in *The Crown of Life,* where he points out that every major religion seems to emphasize the power of "the word" in regard to when God was and is creating the Earth. In St. John in The Bible it states: "In the beginning was the Word and the Word was with God and the Word was God". Thus as we utter words ourselves, and especially the sacred words, we become creators or co-creators likewise, of the energies and presence of God!

The sounds "Aum" and "Om", from the ancient Hindu texts, have been acknowledged as God's sacred sounds of creation in the East. These sounds are known as a conduit through which we can access the God energies. There seems to be confusion and disagreement as to whether these sounds are interchangeable and/or contradictory to each other. Recently it was revealed to the author, that "Aum", the sacred sound of creation, imitates the energies of God to those who repeat it over and over. And "Om", another sacred sound, will sustain the initiated energy created from "Aum", if we switch to "Om" and repeat it again and again.

So as we utter "Aum", we would usually begin to feel the God energies via tingling, and/or chills, and/or heat, and/or a vibratory sensation, and/or a sense of euphoria in the head or hands or heart or spinal column or combinations of these. And then once this energy is catalyzed by "Aum", we switch to repeating "Om" to keep the flowing of the God energy anchored in us. Again, it is worthy of mentioning that the sensation of such energy is relative since God's energy is always present with us in some form or forms. But these methods being discussed are more powerful ways to really feel the life force energies of God.

The most sacred mantra in the East, and maybe on the entire Earth, is the "GAYATRI MANTRA". Its origin can be traced back at least twelve thousand years. Although the Gayatri Mantra is difficult to learn for several reasons, it is more than worth the effort since it very powerfully manifests the presence of God. The Gayatri Mantra is from the Sanskrit language, probably the most prefect and powerful language we have on the Earth today, AND IT MEANS "PERFECT FORM" Sanskrit is not only a very beautiful and poetic language, the vibrations which are produced by speaking this language aloud are very energizing to the body and calming to the mind and our emotions. A recording of the Gayatri Mantra, recorded by Satchi Sai Baba, is available from Flanagan Research, Box 686, Novato, CA 94947. Since the initial composition of this book, many other beautiful recording have been made of this mantra, including one by Dr. Newton. While the author will reveal the words of the mantra, it is important to have a recording in order that you can produce the proper pronunciation, intonation, and meter so that the full power of the Gayatri can be created. The Gayatri mantra is as follows:

> "Aum Bhur Bhuvah Suvaha,
> Tat Savithur Varenyam,
> Bhargo Devasya Dheemahi,
> Dhiyo Yonah Prachodayath."

So powerful are the vibrations from this mantra in producing and/ or attracting the life force energies, that when sand is placed on a table and the vibrations produced by people repeating it are applied to the table, the nine sacred geometric symbols of God displayed in the Hindu Mandala are created on the table top, which are included in the "SHREE YANTRA". This Yantra is a symbolic representation of God and of the atomic regions of existence and creation.

Another powerful Eastern Mantra is: "Om Mani Padme Hum." Translated, this means God is the power and truth. Swami Satchidananda favors the "Hari Om" Mantra, which invokes the cosmic consciousness of God to remove obstacles and barriers that prevent us from knowing God better. Still another powerful mantra from the Hebrew is the "Kodoish" Mantra as set forth in *The Keys of Enoch,* by Dr. J.J. Hurtak. A recording of this mantra is available from The Academy for Future Science, P.O. Box FE, Los Gatos, CA 95031.

Still another powerful mantra which can be repeated in English and thus is more familiar for us is the "Christ, reveal thyself!" mantra. If this is repeated again and again, the presence of the Christ can often be materialized and felt very profoundly, especially in the heart area. And, when this mantra is repeated by a group of people, the Christ energies generated, which are a portal through which we may find God, can powerfully invoke God's presence. The same results can ensue from invoking other masters such as Krishna, Ram, Babaji Nagaraj, Buddha, Arch Angel Michael, Asclepius, etc. There are other powerful Sanskrit Mantras listed in Dr. Newton's new book, *A MAP TO HEALING AND YOUR ESSENTIAL DIVINITY.*

Any and all MANTRAS SHOULD BE REPEATED AT LEAST 108 TIMES CONSECUTIVELY TO GET THE FULL EFFECT AND THE MOST BENEFIT THEREFROM! If you cannot do 108 repetitions, then speak them at least sixteen consecutive times.

Also, using one or more of the sacred names of God in a mantra, can powerfully invoke God's presence. *THE SEVENTY TWO SACRED NAMES OF GOD* are listed in *The Wisdom of the Ages,* by Manly P. Hall. These sacred names would include YHWH (YahWeh), Elohim, Jehovah, etc. Another aspect of these sacred names are *The Seventy Two Names of God* from *Exodus* of *The Bible*, as is discussed in detail in Dr. Newton's, *A Map to Healing and Your Essential Divinity.* Mantras work in the same manner as affirmations and subliminal tapes. They reprogram the subconscious mind, more closely aligning us with God. The more they are repeated the more effectively and powerfully they work. But with the sacred mantras, such as the Gayatri, it must again be emphasized that pronunciation and meter are imperative to maximizing the potential in the mantra.

There may be some readers who are having trouble meditating despite all the information and techniques given in this chapter. For those people, there is a cassette tape set titled "Ultra Meditation", by Zygon Industries, which is guaranteed to produce the Alpha and Theta brain levels/consciousness, which allow meditation to occur. This now know as "Mind Tech" and "Super Life". The newest CD's are known as "Ultra Meditation: The Five Steps to Transcendence", by Dane Spotts.

Let us now investigate subliminal reprogramming of the brain and Neurolinguistic Programming, in the next chapter, after partaking of the exercise below.

EXERCISE

Use one of the mantras listed or create your own mantra or invoke one of the special names of God or one of those "masters" serving God, and repeat it again and again, at least 108 times for maximum effect. The mantra can be a focus of your meditation. Many people just use the word of God's creation, "AUM" or "OM" for their first meditation. By performing DIAPHARAMATIC BREATHING, you will be able to relax more completely and in so doing you will feel God's presence sooner and more intensely. After you feel this presence through one or more of the symptoms of God, which can be tingling, chills, heat, warmth or vibration—in one or more parts of your body including the head, hands, heart, or spinal column—you can feel the "God presence" building in intensity so long as you remain relaxed.

If you can do this in a group format, such as with a meditation group, the results of the "God effect" will be much more easily and quickly achieved and more powerful, likewise. Be aware of any and all things that occur to you during your meditational experience and note any messages or directions which God or "teachers" may be imparting to you!

CHAPTER 4

Subliminal And Neurolinguistic Programming Of The Human Mind

The phrase "Play it again, Sam", has a relevance in our lives since our SUBCONSIOUS MIND/COMPUTER is CONSTANTLY "PLAYING AGAIN" the "BROKEN RECORD" NEGATIVE EXPERIENCES FROM OUR PAST and most of us are not even aware of this. The subconscious mind, of course, is an invaluable and essential element in the controlling of our autonomic nervous system. The autonomic-nervous system is constantly guiding and adjusting our heart and cardiovascular system, our breathing, and controlling the central nervous system, among other things. If you had to use your conscious mind to perform these functions, you would probably be overwhelmed with all of these vital responsibilities, and even if you were not overwhelmed, you would have little time to do anything else other than perform these life sustaining functions. So, it is self evident that the subconscious mind is indispensable to us.

The subconscious mind is also an extremely sophisticated computer system, more elaborate than any computer man has ever built. Literally everything which has happened in your life is stored in your "computer"/ subconscious. Figures of the capacity of this "computer" to perceive and store information run anywhere from the logging of one million to ten million individual pieces of information per second, per day, twenty four hours a day. This "computer", however, is unlike any other computer in that it retrieves information from your past whether you desire this information or not. The scope of this "computer" includes precognitive childhood experiences and past lifetimes!

If this seems outrageous, then consider the following questions. Why do people have phobias which cannot be related to any conscious event which has transpired in their life? Why do people keep experiencing the same problems in their lives, again and again? How do people just have "natural abilities" in some areas and be so inept in other areas in their lives? Why do you hate some people whom you meet immediately for no logical reason? Why do you get along with or love some people deeply the first instant you meet them?

The answers to all of these questions relates to the stored memories in your "computer"/subconscious mind from this and previous lifetimes. As Dr. Eldon Taylor relates in *Subliminal Learning: An Eclectic Approach,* we are in reality *prisoners of our minds.* Dr. Taylor has discovered that our memories influence our thoughts and actions, contrary to the belief that our thoughts control the experiencing of our lives. In many instances, we are as imprisoned by our past experiences as Pavlov's salivating dog! Thus the things which we would like to do, we often cannot perform, and those things which we do not want to do, we do, to paraphrase a passage from the Bible.

EXPERIENCES HAVE SEPARATED US FROM A CONSCIOUS RECOLLECTION OF GOD! This is even true even when we want to know that God is our "salvation" and EVEN THOUGH GOD IS AN OMNIPRESENCE (always present with us)! The real problem is that it is very hard for most of us to access this "separating" information in our "computer"/sub-consciousness/brain. WE DO NOT HAVE THE REPROGRAMMING ALGORIHMS, in a manner of speaking.

Fortunately, due to extensive research into the brain and other related fields, we now know how to deprogram "separating programs" and install the programs of "oneness/integration" with our Creator. THE EASIEST WAY TO DO THIS IS SUBLIMINALLY! Subliminal reprogramming often succeeds where other methods fail. This is because the subconscious mind has a memory saving function which makes it very difficult to install new information which is contradictory to existing data in your brain. By bombarding the subconscious mind with messages below the conscious perceptual threshold, Dr. Taylor and other subliminal research have show that such information is more readily accepted and stored in the computer-brain.

Subliminal messages can be projected either visually or orally. By using an oral mode of transmission, subliminal tapes/CD's can be listened to while sleeping, eating, studying, exercising, etc. To get a substantial more benefit from subliminal messages, they must be played at least once, daily, for thirty consecutive days. Enhanced effectiveness in subliminal retention is realized by listening to them with stereo headphones.

While it is true that subliminal messages are not exactly a self induced method to invoke God consciousness, they are included in this section because they are so closely related to the previous chapter and subsequent information to follow The thirty consecutive day requirement for optimal subliminal assimilation and more profound effectiveness can be shortened considerably when these tapes are played at night on an auto-reversing tape or CD player. Usually profound results will ensue after a week or so of this concentrated subliminal approach. This was discovered by Dr. Eldon Taylor at Progressive Awareness Research and by Brother Charles at the MSH Foundation.

Without reservation, the author can recommend the tapes from Dr. Taylor at Progressive Awareness Research, which number more than a hundred. The tapes will remove the "wedges" and "blocks" that separate ourselves and God. For accessing more God consciousness, the following tapes are recommended: "Spiritual Healing", "Love, Light and Life", and "Using the Force". These messages begin to unleash our divinity so that God is a naturally occurring phenomenon in our life—not just the occasional contact that most of us make—if ever!

There are also other ways to reprogram the computer-brain/mind and the most effective of these is Neuro-Linguistic Programming (NLP). While NLP can allow us to think more realistically and clearly, it also has a mind reprogramming technique called "swishing". "Swishing" is used when we have uncovered a "wedge" or "blockage" in our lives which is interfering with the full enjoyment of living. Let us say, for example, that we have made the realization that we feel God does not really love us. By the technique of "swishing" we can visualize a picture of God (perhaps as an intense light or fire), and ourselves with God, with God showing no in need for or interest in us. Then we would frame this visualization within a picture frame. We would then create a picture of how we would like our relationship to be with God in the lower left hand corner of our picture frame.

Next, take the original picture and see it becoming very hazy and indistinct and as this is occurring we move the new picture from the lower left hand corner to the center of the picture frame. As it reaches the center, see the new picture becoming larger and larger, filling the entire picture frame as you see the old picture completely fade away. Then tell your mind that you have released the old pattern and you wish to substitute the new pattern just framed. As in subliminal tapes or affirmations and mantras, to get the full effectiveness of the "swishing" reprogramming, using this process for at least thirty consecutive days, brings the best and most lasting results. A very good book detailing NLP is *Using Your Brain—For A Change,* by Richard Bandler. It would be highly advantageous for most people to become more familiar with the communication and mind functioning concepts of NLP.

Neurolinguistiic Programming "Swishing" Technique

Make a picture in your head of some situation you wish to change in your mind.

Old Program

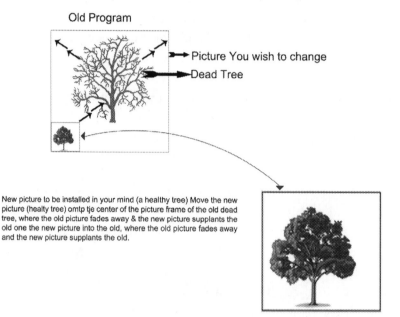

→ Picture You wish to change

→ Dead Tree

New picture to be installed in your mind (a healthy tree) Move the new picture (healty tree) omtp tje center of the picture frame of the old dead tree, where the old picture fades away & the new picture supplants the old one the new picture into the old, where the old picture fades away and the new picture supplants the old.

(New program has replaced the old program)

Diagram # 2

This will work with health issues, business, and prosperity.

ALSO, CHECK THE "THETA CONSCIOUSNESS HEALING" PROTOCOLS IN CHAPTER FOUR OF "A MAP TO HEALING AND YOUR ESSENTIAL DIVINITY", by Dr. Newton. This is an incredibly quick and highly effective protocol for deprogramming and reprogramming the subconscious/computer-brain/mind! In fact, the "swishing" technique can be integrated into "Theta Healing" and Theta Consciousness Healing" protocols, as discussed in Dr. Newton's other book.

EXERCISE

Take some problem that recurs in your life and use the NLP technique discussed above to begin to reprogram your brain.

EXERCISE

If you are really serious about changing things in your life, begin to work with subliminal tapes according to the instructions in this chapter. You can use more than one tape per day, as long as you follow the thirty day requirement for each one, or use the auto-reverse tape playing techniques each night for at least month, for faster results.

CHAPTER 5

Toning, Singing, And Related Concepts To Attune To God

Closely related to mantras, are hymns. The idea is "to make a joyful noise unto the Lord". The most powerful hymns to which the author has been exposed are those written by Mary Baker Eddy contained in the *Christian Science Hymnal*. So powerfully do these hymns focus the "life force" energies, also known as Prana or Chi or "God force", so that many times you can feel "chills" or electricity going down your spine while they are being sung. And it is this effect of the "chills" and electricity which is proof that you are powerfully encountering your Creator because of the electrical bio-feedback!

Many people have also found that great classical music such as that produced by Beethoven, Brahms, and Bach, among others, are spiritually imbued with the force of God. Similar results are also often produced by listening to Baroque music and modern classics such as Pachelbel as well as New Age music such as that produced by Kitaro, Stephen Halperin, Paul Horn, Vangelis, Jean-Luc Ponty, Keith Jarrett, to name a few.

Specific tapes the author have often used to more powerfully invoke the God energies are: "Tibetan Plateau", by David Parsons; "Planetary Unfolding", by Michael Stearns; "Open Mind", by Jean-Luc Ponty;

"Sacred Space Music", by Constance Demby; "Morning Star", through Mahoteh; "Opera Sauvage" by Vangelis; the "Fresh Air" series of tapes by Manheim Steamroller; and "The Koln Concert" and "The Vienna Concert" by Keith Jarrett.

These various music's discussed are effective because they effectuate a relaxation and stimulate the production of endorphins (discussed in detail in the chapter devoted to endorphins) which causes the electromagnetic energy field around our bodies to be become more fully charged. This in turn creates the conditions by which God can touch us more profoundly with the life force energies. The music's which many people believe to give us the least access to God are "hard rock", and disorganized types of progressive jazz. For some people, syncopated music is also disruptive to experiencing the God presence. However, Dr. Newton has discovered that these types of music can actually induce a "Theta Consciousness"/ God Consciousness. Certainly music which has repetitive elements contained therein will really transport us to the "THETA REALM" and "TRANCE CONSCIOUSNESS. THESE ARE THE LEVELS WHERE WE REALLY REACH AN ATTUNEMENT WITH GOD. This is discussed more fully in Chapter Three, among others, in *A Map to Healing and Your Essential Divinity: The Physics of the Immortal "Light Body" and the Creator's Template of Perfection for his Peoples!,* by Dr. Newton

Toning is an even more powerful method than music by which to invoke the God energies, since you are creating the vibrations yourself. TONING is done with the voice like singing, but instead of trying to produce perfect notes and pitches, the emphasis is on CREATING RESONANCE, VIBRATIONS, and OVERTONES. The idea in toning is to make the mouth a resonating chamber. This is done by closing the soft palate in the mouth against the lower throat wall and closing off the nasal passages as much as possible. You then fill the diaphram fully with air and begin to form the actual sounds described. (This will be discussed in more detail in the chapter on breathing techniques.)

Vowel sounds usually give the most powerful toning vibrations for most people as well as the consonant sounds of "L" and "R". Powerful vowel-consonant combinations include "LA", "RA", "LE", and "RE". The "RE" sound, emphasizing the "E" the most, is particularly powerful in that it appears to stimulate the Pineal and Pituitary Glands. The author has created a toning tape concentrating on the above combinations of sounds, which can activate the Pituitary and Pineal Glands. These glands secrete chemicals which cause the brain/mind to be more spiritually receptive, thus more open to God. Also, very powerful toning is achieved through split level or octave toning such as has been practiced by Tibetan monks for thousands of years. There is a recording of this type of toning called "Tantric Harmonics", by the Tibetan Gyume Tantric Monks. As discomforting or inharmonious as many people may find the "Tantric Harmonics" recording, those people who will just experience the tape and not judge what is going on, will often be rewarded with a powerful encounter with God. The Tibetans have been doing this type of toning for thousands of years.

Remember, THE GOAL IN TONING IS NOT TO PRODUCE BEAUTIFUL, PERFECT SOUNDS BUT RATHER TO CREATE AS MUCH RESONANCE, overtones, and vibrations as possible. If you get beautiful tones in the process, that is an added bonus. Oftentimes, in a group toning session, the notes produced by the various participants start off being inharmonious. However, after some time has passed, invariably a HARMONIUS SYNCHRONICITY will be created among the group. Invaluable books on toning are: "Toning: The creative Power of the Voice", by Laurel Elizabeth Keyes, and "Sound Medicine", by Leah Maggie Garfield. Another powerful toning tape/CD is: "On Hearing Solar Winds", by David Hykes and the Harmonic Choir. This is the most powerful example of beautiful toning the author has ever experienced. It creates a very relaxed and ethereal feeling. Also a very good example of beautiful toning is the Brother Charles tapes distributed by the MSH Foundation and Paul Horn's, "Inside the Great Pyramid", which alternates between the flute and toning.

Toning effectuates the presence of God in much the same manner as music. There is the effect of altered brainwaves in the alpha, theta, and delta spectrum, which more naturally attunes us to God. Again, a relaxation is created in the body that allows God to more fully permeate our body and soul. Anthropologically, toning, chanting, and singing can be traced back to "primitive man". They were a way to release emotions and stress, and to more effectively deal with fearful situations.

The ENDORPHINS which can be generated from toning make us more receptive, emotionally and mentally, to detecting God's presence. The increased electromagnetic energy which we generate when we are relaxed is a "NATURAL MAGNET" which attracts God—unfailingly—whether you sense it or not. These electromagnetic energies are manifested around the body as ethers and auras which are synonymous with a halo. Those people who have developed psychic/etheric vision can literally "see" this phenomenon occurring. Again, this can be related to the halo effect depicted around Jesus in paintings, especially the picture of Jesus by Nanette M. A. Crist.

Realize, too, that singing, though not as powerful as toning in charging the etheric energies in the body, is also a good way to achieve the same result with lesser intensity. If you will begin to notice, you might observe that people who are "always singing" are usually happier people than those who do not sing very much. Singing, then, creates a joyousness which again, naturally attracts "God Consciousness".

Tibetan bowls, bells, cymbals, and gongs (collectively known as Tibetan instruments) create this effect as powerfully, if not more so, than toning. The Tibetan bells and bowls are played by "running" a dowel around their outer perimeter. When these Tibetan instruments are activated, they release highly energized resonating, overtone sounds which penetrate and relax the bodies of most people. These effects are accentuated the most when the Tibetan instruments are formulated from a special blend of seven formulated metals. The five metal formulations are still very good but not as powerful as the seven blends, and the three metal blends create less of an effect than the five blends. Also, the "crystal bowls" which have been created in the last few years will generate the

God energies similar to the Tibetan instruments. A good example of the sounds created by Tibetan instruments is on the "Tibetan Bells II" tape by Wolff and Hennings.

When Tibetan instruments are used in a group format where you have several instruments being played simultaneously, the God evoking qualities of these instruments is significantly increased. And, when toning in either a solo or group format is combined with Tibetan instruments and/or in conjunction with toning tapes such as "On Hearing Solar Winds", the life force energies of God are summoned forth even more substantially. These energies are felt more intensely because of the INCREASED NUMBERS OF VIBRATIONS (waveforms) BEING PRODUCED. These create a GREATER RELAXATION IN THE BODY that leads to elevated electromagnetic energies and waveforms emanating from God and the "atomic field", which penetrate and enliven the cells in our bodies with God's presence.

However, sometimes people will experience a headache or a physical or emotional uneasiness when first subjected to toning or Tibetan instruments. These negative conditions can almost always be attributed to the fact that the person experiencing these effects is resisting the sounds produced. This resistance can be overcome by simply relaxing, such as diaphragmatic breathing, and allowing your body to be bathed by the sound produced. In such a nonreactive state of being, these problems should be eliminated allowing you to reap the benefits of a closer relationship with God.

The individual notes of the musical scale also have an enervating effect and a direct interrelationship with the Chakras (energy centers) on the body. There are seven major Chakras and at least eight minor chakras. Especially with the Heart through Crown and the Hand Chakras, are the energy centers by which God can be more profoundly accessed. Refer to the chart below for the location of the identified Chakras.

The following chart specifically relates each note of the musical scale to the Chakras. If you were feeling unsettled or upset about something, it would manifest in one or more of the Chakras. By reproducing the appropriate note or notes, it is possible to dispel sickness, stress, emotional trauma, and mental trauma. When you eliminate these things, the "wedges" that prevent us from more fully experiencing God are removed.

MUSICAL SCALE:
NOTE INTER-RELATIONSHIP WITH THE CHAKRAS

MAJOR CHAKRAS	SOUND	NOTE	MINOR CHAKRAS
Crown	Silence	B	Shoulder
Brow	Aum	A	Elbow
Throat	Ah/Hum	G	Hand
Heart	Hum/Eyam	F	Hip
Solar Plexus	Ram	E	Knee
Spleenic	Vom	D	Ankle
Root	Lum	C	Foot

Some of the information on the chart above comes from *Harmonies of Tones and Colors,* by Hughes; *Scientific Basis and Build of Music,* by Ramsay; and from the article "Law of Cycles", by Dale Pond in Volume Four, Issue Eleven of "Sympathetic Vibratory Physics". It also comes from the work of John Keely, a musician/scientist.

The Chart which follows lists general pitch relationship to the Chakra System. You will find, from experimentation, that you can feel, from the vibrations which emanate, a vast difference in how different pitches physically affect Chakras. The lower the pitch, the lower the Chakra affected. The higher the pitch, the higher the Chakra affected.

GENERAL PITCH RELATIONSHIP TO THE CHAKRA SYSTEM

MAJOR CHAKRAS	RELATIVE PITCH	MINOR CHAKRAS
Crown	highest (soprano/falsetto)	Shoulder
Brow	high (between soprano & falsetto)	Elbow
Throat	middle high(alto) low	Hand
Heart	middle (tenor)	Hip
Solar Plexus	middle low (baritone)	Knee
Spleenic	low (between baritone & bass)	Ankle
Root	lowest (bass)	Foot

After some personal experience, you will know from the vibrational feedback, such as tingling, chills, warmth, heat, electricity or actual vibration, which pitches affect which Chakras. Pitch or notes alone, are powerful ways to activate the chakras and thus make oneself more receptive to the "God Energies"/Prana. This is because the Chakras are very concentrated vortexes of electromagnetic energy. And since these energies are the essence of God and likewise ourselves, there is a NATURALLY OCCURRING SYMPATHETIC RESONANCE which allows a merging between God and our Chakras (part of our energy field and interrelated to Meridians and Nadis).

THIS SYMPATHETIC RESONANCE IS MAGNIFIED WHEN BOTH THE APPROPRIATE PITCH AND NOTE ARE APPLIED SIMULTANEOUSLY TO THE CHAKRA! While this explanation may seem remote and even unrelated, on an experiential level the merging of these electromagnetic energies between God and us, can be intense and lead to euphoric states of God Consciousness.

It is also known that each note of the scale corresponds to a specific color of the spectrum, and each color relates to a specific numerological vibration which is determined by your day of birth. Thus, there will be a note of the scale which will calm and balance your emotions, putting you in a relaxed state and more receptive to God. This is considerably confirmed by the research of Sharry Edwards and her "Sound Signature" protocols of diatonic musical note healing at the subwoofer level.

Realize, however, that notes emanating from brass instruments, being an aggregate of enharmonic waves, and string instruments, a combination of harmonic waves, will have a dramatically different effect on the body, emotions and mind. In general, brass instruments stir and open things whereas string instruments synthesize and are very calming. The Tibetan instruments combine aspect of both brass and string instruments and thus can both open emotions for examination and allow them to be synthesized, calmed and reformed so that we can function on a higher spiritual level, in the Theta/Divine consciousness range.

As regarding the diatonic scale, red resonates with "C", orange with "D", yellow with "E", green with "F", blue with "G", indigo with "A", and violet with "B". This information comes from *Harmonies of Tones and Colors,* by Hughes, and *Scientific Basis and Build of Music,* by Ramsay as related in "Sympathetic Vibratory Physics" journal in the "Law of Cycles" article by Dale Pond.

We also know how these colors relate to your numerological birth date, as shown in *Chirio's Book of Numbers,* by Chirio. Number one vibration resonates with yellow, number two with green, number three with violet, number four with blue, number five with white (which includes all colors), number six with blue, number seven with green, number eight with indigo, and number nine with red. The way in which you arrive at your birth number is to combine all of the numbers of your numerical date of birth. If you were born on the third of a month, you would be a three vibration; if you were born on the thirteenth, you would be a four vibration; if you were born on the twenty seventh, you would be a nine vibration.

We also know that there are notes which will best balance our number vibration and increase our receptivity to God. Consult the chart below to determine which note and color is the result of your vibration number. With some experimentation, you can also discover which pitch of your numerological note most powerfully invokes God for you. Remember to use your note and color not only for meditation but also when you are experiencing stress or emotional upsets, because these are states of being which prevent us from experiencing God Consciousness!

NUMEROLOGICAL NOTE AND COLOR COMPATIBILITY CHART

NUMBER VIBRATION	NOTE OF SCALE	COLOR
1	E	Yellow
2	F	Green
3	B	Violet
4	G	Blue
5	D & All Notes	Orange/White
6	G	Blue
7	F	Green
8	A	Indigo
9	C	Red

The notes of the scale can be used to stimulate Acupuncture meridians and to stimulate organs other than the endocrine system. This is synthesized in the chart below.

MUSICAL NOTES AS INTERRELATED TO ACUPUNCTURE POINTS AND ORGANS OTHER THAN THE ENDOCRINE SYSTEM.

NOTE:	ACUPUNCTURE POINT:	ORGAN:
A	Triple Warmer	Brain
A#		Spleen
B		Gall Bladder
C	Central Meridian Governing Meridian	Heart
C#		Kidney
D		Pericardium
D#		Liver
E		Lung
F		Small Intestine
F#		Bladder
G		Stomach

Thus, if we desired to make our Brain more receptive to God, by producing the appropriate note, this can be stimulated by making the note "A". The effectiveness of this would be significantly enhanced by producing A at Soprano or Falsetto pitch. (Consult general pitch chart to refresh your memory on the effects of tone and pitch). If we desired to make the Heart more amenable to God, this can be accomplished by producing the note "C". The effectiveness of this note would be increased through using a Tenor pitch. In general, if there is an organ in the body which is malfunctioning, by creating the proper musical note, we can often restore it to a more optimal state. The benefit to us is not only better health, but also a better attunement and atonement with God, since sickness and disease usually create "wedges" and "blockages" that significantly reduce the presence of God's Life Force Energies/Prana/Chi!.

We will next consider the value of colors in attracting the power and presence of God after you review and perform the next exercise.

EXERCISE _____

Begin using the toning sounds to initiate a meditation session. Do not worry about how "nice" the tones are, and do not worry whether they are melodious. Just let the sounds come randomly from your mouth as an echo chamber, remembering to close off the throat with the tongue touching the soft palate (right after the hard part of your upper mouth) so as to block off the nasal passages. Concentrate on producing resonating overtones in the hollow of your mouth. Give your attention to producing vowel sounds and the "RA", "LA", "RE", "LE" sounds. Also, experiment with pitch in your toning and notice how varying the pitch affects you and your energy (chakra) centers. As you do this, be aware of your feelings of God—tingling, chills, warmth or heat, electricity and/or vibration—in the head, hands, heart, or spinal column. As you begin to sense the presence and augmentation of God's energies, you can cease toning and let yourself drift into meditation. Be aware of what is happening to you during your meditation and be cognizant of any messages or directions which God may be sending you.

As an alternative, tone the musical note which corresponds with your numerological vibration. Experiment with various pitches and see which pitch or pitches calm, balance, and relax you. Be aware of the same sensations and feedback you might experience as outlined in the previous exercise.

CHAPTER 6

Using Color To Harmonize With God

In reality, color is just an illusion. This is discussed in *Color and the Edgar Cayce Readings,* by Roger Lewis, as well as the fact that color is really just energy of different "wave types". Although the colors of these energies may be illusive, the vibrations emanating from these energy waves are very real and have a definite effect on us. These electromagnetic vibrations of the colors are one and the same with God, according to the Edgar Cayce readings.

Cayce also brought through the information that tone (musical notes) and color coordinate the forces of the body so that it can create a perfectly functioning organism. These same properties of color and tone which synchronize the bodily functions, promote spiritual growth as well as mental clarity and emotional balance. Furthermore, as was discussed in the previous chapter, Cayce said that colors are directly interrelated to and affect the chakra and endocrine system. In an overall sense, then, COLOR HELPS US HARMONIZE WITH GOD, no matter what our level of spiritual development. It is this harmonizing with God, such as through color or sound, which reveals the pathway to knowing God on an experiential basis.

Let us now examine the energies of each color, individually. Violet is associated with the Crown Chakra, the pituitary gland, and the planet Jupiter. The pituitary affects all of the other endocrine glands and awakens and directs spiritual understanding and growth. The properties of color to invoke the presence of God, have been known for thousands of years. One thing to guard against, however, is allowing the negative forces of the color violet—namely aloofness, vanity, and desiring adoration—to overcome the spiritual qualities of violet.

When the pituitary gland is opened in meditations, using the color violet, the color often changes from violet to gold in those people more spiritually advanced. Gold then, is another color associated with God. It has much the same properties as violet. When this color transformation occurs, there is an "inner silence" which allows us to hear the "voice of God", according to Cayce and the author's personal experiences. Thus the energy emanated from violet, purple, and gold powerfully catalyze the energies of God through the Crown Chakra!

Indigo is the color associated with the Brow Chakra, the pineal gland, and the planet Mercury. This is an important spiritual color in that it stimulates the pineal gland which works in conjunction with the pituitary gland in raising our spirituality and our searching for God. However, non-spiritual aspirants will not prefer, or feel comfortable with indigo, since it makes people uncomfortable who are out of balance and control of their emotions and thoughts. This is discussed in more detail in *Color and the Edgar Cayce Readings*.

Blue is associated with the Throat Chakra, the thyroid gland, and the planet Uranus. Blue is also secondarily associated with the Brow Chakra, the pineal gland, and is a calming color. As Edgar Cayce related, it is the color of spiritual awareness and aspirations. This is a good color through which to access the Christ energies, as well as the Buddhic and other "Master" type energies. The focusing on the color blue to accentuate the "lower passions" will often bring eventual hardship. But, by using this color to effectuate personality changes, we can bring our will into a closer alignment with God and thus feel more fully access the energy of our Creator.

Green is associated with the Heart Chakra, the thymus gland, and the planet Venus. Cayce also attributed love, healing, health, praise, and thanksgiving, as part of the vibrational properties of this color. Green, with blue tinges as opposed to yellow tinges, will be more powerful in invoking and experiencing God through the heart. Pink is also associated with the Heart Chakra. Although pink does not have the healing/health energies of green, it is nevertheless very powerful in relaxing and opening the heart so that we can experience God's abundant love!

Yellow is the color associated with the Solar Plexus Chakra, the adrenal glands, and the planet Mars. While the color yellow affects our bodily metabolism and fears, we are most interested in it because of the joy and happiness it can elicit in us. Such joy and happiness puts us in a more receptive state of being to experience God's energies. Yellow is also associated with innovation, imagination, and sexuality.

The color orange is represented by the Spleenic Chakra, the spleen, and the planet Neptune. While orange is also associated with sexuality, we are interested in it for the properties Edgar Cayce attributed to orange—namely spiritual insight, spiritual development, and mystic and psychic experiences. Orange with tinges of brown should be avoided since it stimulates lack of ambition and lack of caring, whereas golden orange elicits vitality and self control.

Red is synonymous with the Base Chakra, the gonads, and the planet Saturn. Red, as well as orange and yellow, will also catalyze the sexual energies, much more powerfully than either yellow or orange. Red is also associated with anger and aggression. Its most positive aspects are for the activation of creativity and the powerful distribution of God's life force energies throughout our bodies. Other than the overall vitality it creates for us and the numerological significance red has for number nine personality types, red is not normally a color used to unleash spiritual tendencies!

Now let us examine some additional colors. White is associated with the Crown Chakra. However, since it contains all colors, it will activate all of the Chakras with an equal effectiveness. Silver combines some of the qualities of violet, indigo, and blue, being spiritually uplifting and connecting with God. It can activate the mental centers and the absence of all colors, and as such, affects all of the Chakras and Endocrine Glands. Black is invaluable in absorbing and removing emotional hurt and negativity, the "wedges" that prevent us from significantly experiencing God.

Now, how do we use these colors in light of the fact that EDGAR CAYCE ATRRIBUTED AS MUCH POTENTIAL HEALING POWER TO COLOR AS TO MEDICINE? One way we can influence ourselves with color is by wearing them on our clothes or surrounding ourselves with them in interior environments (house, office, etc.). Also, the Chakras and various parts of the body can be activated through the directing of colored lights at them, as in the "Dinsbaugh Healing" protocols.

Another way to use color is through wearing or carrying colored gemstones on or close to our bodies. The following information will be detailed in depth in the chapters on the spiritual properties of crystals and gemstones, but as a quick reference for this chapter, if we desired to stimulate the God energies through our Crown Chakra, we would use such purple minerals as Amethyst Quartz, Sugilite (Lavulite), Charoite, or possibly Lepidolite since they radiate the vibrational energies of violet/purple/lavender. We could either place these minerals on top of our heads or hold them in our hands to receive the vibrational qualities of God from these colors, which are reinforced by the activation of the pituitary gland.

A SYNTHESIZED COLOR CHART IS PROVIDED ON THE NEXT PAGE:

SYNTHESIZED COLOR CHART:

COLOR	CHAKRA AFFEC'T'ED	GLANDS AFFECTED	GOD QUALITIES
Violet	Crown (Secondary Brow)	Pituitary	Synonymous with God/silence, through which God is heard
Indigo	Brow	Pineal	Gives access to the violet/purple energy
Blue	Throat/Brow	Thyroid/Pineal	Spiritual aspirations and uplifting Christ Consciousness
Green	Heart	Thymus	Healing/balance/love/thanksgiving
Yellow	Solar Plexus	Adrenals	Happiness/joy
Orange	Spleenic	Spleen	Spiritual insight and development
Red	Root	Gonads	Creativity
Gold	Crown	Pituitary	Same as Violet
Silver	Crown/Brow	Pituitary/Pineal	Similar to violet/Indigo
Pink	Heart	Thymus	Love
White	Crown/all	Pituitary/all	Embodies all Properties
Black	All	All	Absorbs hurts and Negativity

EXERCISES TO PERFORM ARE ON THE NEXT PAGE.

EXERCISE _____

Within your mind, create balls of the colors Violet, Purple, Gold, White, Silver, Indigo, Blue, Green, and Pink, and Black. Individually, one by one, visually place these colors over the corresponding chakras (use chart above). Take your time and note any and all sensations and experiences that transpire while you are doing this.

EXERCISE _____

Take either a ball of Violet, Purple, Gold, or White and place it visually over your Crown Chakra. Then concurrently, take a ball of Indigo or Blue and place it over the Brow Chakra. At the same time, take a ball of Blue light and place it over the Throat Chakra. And in the same process, take a ball of Green or Pink over the Heart Chakra and allow yourself to experience all these colors simultaneously. Note any sensations and experiences that occur after doing this for five to fifteen minutes. This is also another way to begin a meditation session.

EXERCISE _____

Now take each color corresponding to the seven Chakras and place them accordingly in a concurrent manner. Note anything that might transpire. Do you feel calm and balanced after doing this for five minutes? Fifteen minutes?

EXERCISE _____

When you are experiencing a "broken heart", place a ball of black over your Heart Chakra. Do you feel better after five minutes? If not, add a Black ball over the Solar Plexus Chakra. If you are feeling angry, take a ball of Black and place it over the Solar Plexus Chakra. Do you feel calmer after doing this for five minutes? Fifteen minutes?

CHAPTER 7

Breathing Techniques— A Pathway To Relaxation

For most of us, it is not obvious why we do not breathe correctly. As has been previously stated many times already, when we eliminate stress from our lives and learn to *relax,* God's presence becomes more known to us. The easiest method to induce relaxation in the body is through full, diaphragmatic breathing. If you are a singer or a wind instrument performer, you already have developed this essential method of breathing. However, even people who are trained to breathe properly because of their musical abilities, rarely breathe in the diaphragmatic manner on any regular basis other than during performing.

Why is this so? One reason is that stress and emotional trauma cause us to tense up our muscles in the body which almost invariably causes us to breathe very shallow and/or into the chest. ALSO ON A SUBCONSCIOUS LEVEL, THERE ARE STRONG INDICATIONS THAT WE DO NOT WANT TO BE HERE ON EARTH! On a conscious level there will be those people who disagree with this vociferously. However, when these same people are regressed hypnotically, most likely the subconscious mind would validate the accuracy of not wanting to be here. Because of this, we breathe ineffectively and in an unhealthful manner as a symbolic gesture of our protest for being here on Earth! The problem with this is that we cut ourselves off from God by lethargic breathing. As Rajneesh (Osho) has related in *The Book of the Secrets,* proper breathing is the "bridge" to the Universe (which of course is God).

Even during, or just after a stressful event in our lives, we can begin to ELIMINATE and induce relaxation through DIAPHRAGMATIC BREATHING. This simple procedure is accomplished by taking our breath to the area just under our rib cage instead of into our chests. Such a method of breathing has been part of the Eastern religious tradition, especially in the Yogic and Taoist disciplines, for thousands of years and has been known as a pathway to enlightenment—God!

1.

The mechanics of full diaphragmatic breathing are that you inhale the air through your nostrils and instead of through your mouth, and you fill your diaphragm, which is located between your rib cage and stomach. You fill this area as fully as possible with air and then exhale as fully as possible through the nostrils. The easiest way to detect and check if you are breathing diaphragmatic manner, is by putting your hand on your chest and inhale. If the hand raises on the chest, you know that you are not breathing into the diaphragm. If however, repeating this same process but with your hand on the diaphragm and your hand raises during inhalation, you know you are breathing in a diaphragmatic manner.

DIAPHRAGMATIC BREATHING

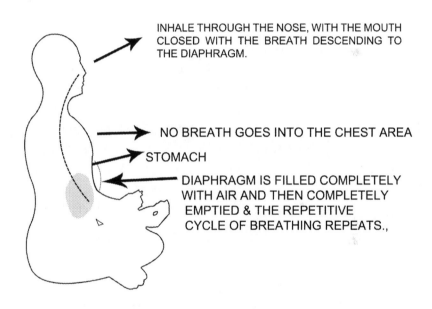

INHALE THROUGH THE NOSE, WITH THE MOUTH CLOSED WITH THE BREATH DESCENDING TO THE DIAPHRAGM.

NO BREATH GOES INTO THE CHEST AREA

STOMACH

DIAPHRAGM IS FILLED COMPLETELY WITH AIR AND THEN COMPLETELY EMPTIED & THE REPETITIVE CYCLE OF BREATHING REPEATS.,

Why full diaphragmatic breathing causes relaxation is not completely known, but we do know that endorphins, powerful chemicals secreted by the brain that create a euphoric feeling and relieve pain, can be released during this type of breathing. We also know that the brain can be entrained into fuller functioning, resulting in more creativity and the ability to assess and better solve problems. Besides this, the body is more completely nourished via the increased oxygen intake from full diaphragmatic breathing. In this manner, your blood and body cells are better nourished. This is discussed in detail in several chapters of Dr. Newton's, *A Map to Healing and Your Essential Divinity.*

The importance of full diaphragmatic breathing cannot be overemphasized. This should be done not only during times of spiritual devotion such as meditation, but also throughout the entire day as much as possible. On a subconscious level, using the three subliminal tapes discussed before, by Progressive Awareness Research, "Spiritual Healing", "Love, Light, and Life", and "Using The Force", will greatly aid in achieving this twenty four hour goal of full diaphragmatic breathing, as well as a fourth tape, "Melting Fat With Metabolism". Again, it should be mentioned that these tapes need to be used at least thirty days consecutively and the greatest efficiency is achieved by using stereo headphones.

During times of spiritual devotion to God, there are breathing techniques which foster a far greater access to God's presence. One of these is the "Breath of Fire". To perform this, you breathe fully into the diaphragm and and exhale in a short staccato pattern. This process is repeated many times over. It can be seen and felt at the diaphragm while being performed. The benefit from this technique is that the brain is entrained into more fully synchronized hemispheric thought patterns by which we are much more likely to sense of the presence and power of God. Even more important is the increase in the electromagnetic energies created by the influx of God's Life Force Energies. This gives us the opportunity to experience the tingling, chills, warmth, vibration, electricity and/or euphoria by which God communicates with us.

Another technique which produces results similar to the "Breath of Fire" is "Alternative Nostril Breathing". It is performed by sealing off one nostril with your finger and inhaling and exhaling into the diaphragm, and on the next breath you seal off the other nostril and inhale and exhale in the same manner. This process is repeated many times over. While performing this, you may begin to feel "light headed". This is a good sign as it indicates you are achieving the altered, fuller brain hemispheric functioning that makes you more receptive to God. This will also provide the generation of the electromagnetic phenomena described for "The Breath of Fire".

Still other breathing techniques are based on repetitious cadence-like breathing such as the 8-8-8-8. By this technique, you inhale your breath diaphragmatically for the count of eight; you hold your breath without exhaling for the count of eight; you exhale over the duration of a count of eight, and you hold your breath without inhaling for the count of eight after exhalation. The process is then repeated over and over. Often there is the same "light headed" feeling as in the "Alternate Nostril Breathing", with the benefits similar as described in the nostril techniques. To achieve an even more euphoric level of God consciousness, you can attempt the 16-16-16-16 count cadence after mastering the 8-8-8-8.

These breathing techniques are thousands of years old and are still effective today. Do not be afraid to develop your own cadence breathing regimens if it seems appropriate for you. And now that we have examined the role of breathing in attracting God more powerfully in our lives, let us consider the use of postures and movements to magnify the power and presence of God in our lives, after the following exercises. Also, PLEASE NOTE THAT THERE ARE SOME PEOPLE WHO FEEL THAT SUCH BREATH CADENCES SUCH AS THE 8-8-8-8, WHERE THERE IS BREATH RETENTION, CLAIM THAT THIS PUTS UNDUE STRESS ON YOUR HEART! Therefore, it may be better to perform the Kriya Yoga Protocols, such as are discussed in Chapter Three of Dr. Newton's other book, "A Map to Healing and Your Essential Divinity".

Also, added as an update to this book, is "The Backflow Meditation", as conceived and named by Chuck (Robert) Schwartz. The two diagrams to follow will explain how this is to be performed. It can be very relaxing and because of this, highly energizing and capable of transporting the practitioner thereof, into a deep Theta consciousness state.

A Map To Healing

Backflow Meditation

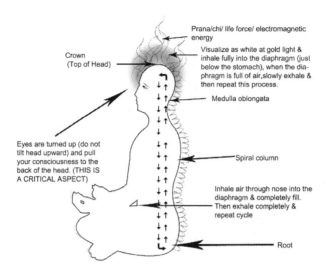

Prana/chi/ life force/ electromagnetic energy

Visualize as white at gold light & inhale fully into the diaphragm (just below the stomach), when the diaphragm is full of air, slowly exhale & then repeat this process.

Crown (Top of Head)

Medulla oblongata

Spiral column

Eyes are turned up (do not tilt head upward) and pull your consciousness to the back of the head. (THIS IS A CRITICAL ASPECT)

Inhale air through nose into the diaphragm & completely fill. Then exhale completely & repeat cycle

Root

Diagram # 4a : Side view

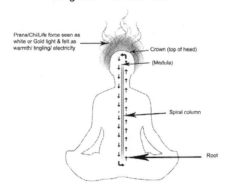

Prana/Chi/Life force seen as white or Gold light & felt as warmth/ tingling/ electricity

Crown (top of head)

(Medula)

Spiral column

Root

Backview of the Backflow Meditation

Use a base meditation posture sitting cross legged on the ground or sit in a chair. See & breathe a column of light and feel the electricity of the Electromagnetic Energy (Prana/Chi/Life Force) causing down into the crown & bending back to the Medula Oblongata down the back of the neck & spinal column & end at the tail bone and then see the energy circulating back up & then down in a continuous cycle.

You will get a "spacey"/trance like feeling from this & that includes a dimensional/consciousness shift into Alpha and Theta consciousness. This is a close replication of how this was taught by Robert(Chuck) Charles Schwrit PULLING YOUR CONSCIOUSNESS TO THE BACK OF YOUR HEAD IS OF CRITICAL IMPORTANCE.

Diagram # 4b

EXERCISE _____

Practice the full diaphragmatic breathing discussed in the beginning of this chapter. Try to make it a regular habit throughout the day. Remember to check yourself on this as many times as possible. You will probably be amazed at how often you find yourself breathing very shallow and/or into only the chest area. When you do, correct yourself. The more you practice diaphragmatic breathing, the more it becomes ingrained into the subconscious mind, thus becoming a habitual process.

EXERCISE _____

After mastering diaphragmatic breathing, begin to experiment with "Breath of Fire", "Alternative Nostril Breathing", or "Cadence" type breathing such as the 8-8-8-8 anytime during the day or to begin a meditation. Be aware of the changes occurring in your consciousness. Are you feeling God more profoundly now? Do you sense any tingling, chills, warmth, vibration, electricity or euphoria?

CHAPTER 8

Postures And Movement Which Invoke Divine Energy

Some of the most powerful encounters the author has had with God on a regular basis is through Tai Chi—especially the Tai Chi "Standing Meditation". The origins of Tai Chi are rooted in Taoism and may go back 2400 years or more. Tai Chi is so effective in giving the body an aerobic exercise and powerfully charging the body with God's electromagnetic energy, that it is the state sanctioned exercise in China today. Originally, the early Communist government in China attempted to outlaw Tai Chi, but was unsuccessful in doing so. It subsequently repealed its earlier ban on Tai Chi and now is officially sanctioned!

The Tai Chi "form" is a series of movements that takes patience to learn and is well worth the effort since it also teaches grace and a profound relaxation as well as the other benefits just listed in this chapter. Learning just the Tai Chi "Standing Meditation" has tremendous benefits to recommend it as a "must do" exercise every day. The standing meditation is a "posture" and involves no movement as does the "form" (a series of movements). However, it probably generates more of God's energy and creates a deeper relaxation than the "form". In fact, the author has been in an air conditioned room of twenty feet by twenty feet with four other people doing the Standing Meditation for fifteen or twenty minutes and every person in the room was not only sweating at the end of the session, but beads of sweat were rolling down all of our faces!!!

The author has never failed in teaching any person how to do the Standing Meditation so that they could get direct feedback from God and feel that God does indeed exist—including skeptics! What is this feeling referred to? It is perceived tingling, chills, warmth, vibrations, electricity or combination of these. However, whereas in the other disciplines that we have covered already, you may not have felt the energy via the symptoms just described, it is almost guaranteed that you will when you perform the Standing Meditation correctly! And, it is very fast and easy to learn.

To perform the "Standing Meditation", face toward magnetic north, stand with your feet about shoulder width apart, with the legs bent at the knees as much as possible and yet still comfortable. The shoulders are sloped forward so that they can be relaxed and thus without tension. Let the hands hang loosely at the outside front of the thighs, yet do not let the hands touch the thighs. To accomplish this, visualize yourself standing in a pool of water, shoulder high, and your hands will just naturally "float" to the right position. The head and neck should be as relaxed as possible with the face looking straight ahead.

Once you begin energizing the body with "Chi", you can turn your hands toward each other and see a positive charge in one hand and a negative charge in the other hands and the hands will be attracted together. But just before the hands touch, change the charge in both hands to either positive-positive or negative-negative and the hands will pull apart. You can repeat this many times and as you do you will feel a ball of energy building in your hands. This is the accumulation of "Chi"!

The attraction and repulsion of the hands should be done in conjunction with breathing in a diaphragmatic manner already described in the chapter on breathing. As you are continuing to do this, close your eyes (not mandatory, but best for most people) and visualize a stream of White or Golden light coming down from God and penetrating your Crown Chakra (refer to the Chakra Chart or Tai Chi diagram that follows, then, see the streaming light begin to build as an ever increasing ball of energy in your Spleenic Chakra. When the ball fills the entire navel area, see it radiating out to all points of the body and especially the hands.

After only a few minutes, most people will feel one or more of the symptoms described in this chapter, but most frequently in the hands and/or face. Your body will be charged with electromagnetic energy—God! At the end of this chapter, there will be a Tai Chi exercise that can give you even more feedback as to the effectiveness of the Standing Meditation. It is recommended that the Standing Mediation be practiced at least three times a day, such as first thing in the morning, midday, and in the evening, for about five to fifteen minutes each session—longer if you desire and really crave living in the "Theta/ Divine Consciousness.

You should also do this at any time you are experiencing any type of disruptive stress in your life. The benefits from this far exceed the effort involved in performing the Standing Meditation. An invaluable book in learning the entire Tai Chi "form" is the "Tai Chi Handbook", by Herman Kauz. Following is a chart depicting the proper elements of the Standing Meditation.

Tai Chi "Standing Meditation"

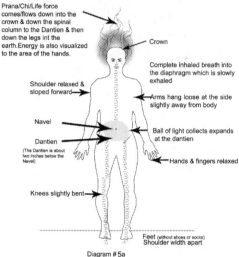

Prana/Chi/Life force comes/flows down into the crown & down the spinal column to the Dantien & then down the legs int the earth.Energy is also visualized to the area of the hands.

Crown

Complete inhaled breath into the diaphragm which is slowly exhaled

Shoulder relaxed & sloped forward→

Arms hang loose at the side slightly away from body

Navel

Ball of light collects expands at the dantien

Dantien

(The Dantien is about two inches below the Navel)

Hands & fingers relaxed

Knees slightly bent→

Feet (without shoes or socks)
Shoulder width apart

Diagram # 5a

E.M. energy & (Prana/Ch/life force) is visualized and breathed diaphragmatically as white or gold light that is pulled down into the crown(TOH) & down the spiral column to the dantien(just below the navel), where a ball of light is created which expands with each inhaled breath. The energy/light is directed down the legs into the earth & grounds you thereto . As the light accumulates, you visualize and breathe it o the exhaled breath throughout the body, including the hands. This will energize the body enough for the next parts of the Standing Meditation

Raising the arms sans muscles (floating arms)

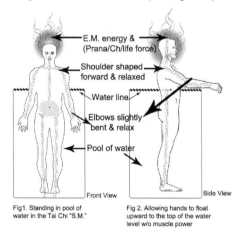

E.M. energy & (Prana/Ch/life force)

Shoulder shaped forward & relaxed

Water line

Elbows slightly bent & relax

Pool of water

Front View

Side View

Fig1. Standing in pool of water in the Tai Chi "S.M."

Fig 2. Allowing hands to float upward to the top of the water level w/o muscle power

Diagram # 5b

You do not actually have to stand in a pool of water. H/E, visualizing such will help your first attempts in using Chi to lift your arms sans muscles. This position can be sustained for a long period of time.

Tai Chi "Standing Meditation"

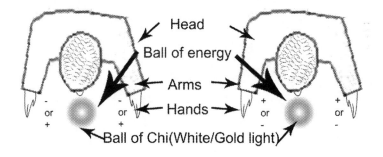

Diagram # 5c : Attraction & Repulsion of the Hands

This attraction & repulsion of the hands is done effortlessly, relaxed & w/o muscles. After getting your hands raised in the imaginary pool of water, in the previous diagram turn the palms of the hands toward each other & separated, see a plus(+) change in one hand & a negative (-) charge in the other hand & the hands will begin to come together. Before the hands come together, see the polarity in the hands becoming plus(+), plus(+) or negative(-),negative(-) & they will push apart. Then repeat the process. As you repeat the attraction – repulsion process, see a ball of parna / white or golden light building in your hands. The hands should become warm &/or with a "tingling" sensation & /or feel currents of electricity. This would be a great "pre-protocol" process for "energy heaters" and message therapists & chiropractors.

Another good way to attract and feel God's presence is through the discipline of Tai Chi Chuh. Although this is not as powerful as the Tai Chi Chuan in invoking God, the Tai Chi Chuh discipline, revealed by Justin Stone, is nevertheless effective and useful. Tai Chi Chuh seems to be a combination of Tai Chi Chuan and Yogic practices. If you are interested in this discipline, the book by Justin Stone describes the designated motions in detail.

Do-In (pronounced DOW-IN), which is Japanese for Tai Chi, is closely related to the Tai Chi Chuan from China, and is almost as powerful, and for some people more so. The methodology to the Do-In Standing Meditation involves the same basic components, except that the hands are hung loosely at the sides of the thighs and the hands are thrust quickly backwards, stopping at a forty five or less degree angle, and returned forward to their original position. (Not forward past the thighs.) This motion is repeated continuously for at least one hundred and eight repetitions. Just remember, you are not moving the hand forward past the thighs on your return stroke. The type and location of the feedback you will receive from God is the same as the Tai Chi Standing Meditation. Following is a diagram depicting the proper procedure of the Do-In "Standing Meditation".

Diagram: 6

Do (Dow)-In Standing Meditation

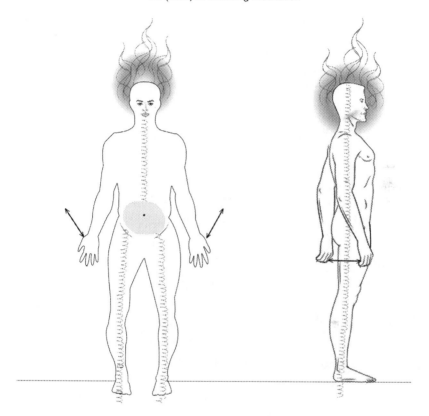

Everything here is the same as the Tai chi "standing meditation". Refer to diagram 3a & 3b.Shoulders are sloped forward & relaxed. Elbows & hands are slightly bent & relaxed, a column of white or gold light is visualized coming down through the head and spinal column into the Dantien and then down the legs & feet & into the ground. As the hands are at the side of the body, slightly separated. There from, push the hands backward, quickly but relaxed,& allow them to come forward but not past parallel to the legs. Repeat this process many repetitions & you will feel the body becoming more energized & the hands also, exhibiting characteristics of warmth, "tingling", electricity. Keep breathing down the column of light & allow to expand the ball of light .

Another Eastern discipline which powerfully invokes God's presence are the various forms of Yoga. While Tai Chi Chuan, is simpler and seems to catalyze the Life Force Energies more rapidly, with Kriya Kundalini Yoga, the author has had significant encounters with God and eliciting Theta/Divine Consciousness! Tantric Yoga, involving sexual energies and Kundalini Yoga can evoke the most powerful Yogic experiences with God's energies. This is why these two types of Yoga were developed—as direct pathways to the Life Force Energies. The specifics of Yoga and more, are covered in detail in Chapter Three of *A Map to Healing and Your Essential Divinity: The Physics of the Immortal 'Light Body' and the Creator's Template of Perfection for His Peoples,* by Dr. Newton.

Still other movements which focus God's energies are Sufi Dancing, rooted in the Islamic tradition, and Feldenkrais, which concentrates on teaching individuals to learn how to move themselves more in harmony with God. Actually, any type of movement, including all types of sports, which are done in a joyous manner, will stimulate the production of endorphins in the brain, creating a more euphoric feeling for us and elevating our consciousness to a level more sympathetic with that of God! Especially useful is walking, which is enhanced by being done in a setting where you are surrounded by nature. Even sexual activity can bring us significantly closer to God if we use the energy created from sex not to only gratify our passions and lust, but rather to use the energies generated to reunite ourselves with God and to glorify the power and presence of God!

The electromagnetic energies which are usually generated from sexual coupling with the opposite sex are an extremely powerful way to experience God, notwithstanding those people who feel that sexual activity is only for procreation or is a debased "lust of the flesh". From Kirilian and Magnetic Field photography, we now have proof of the dramatic increase in the etheric and auric fields around the body following sex. These etheric and auric fields are in at least large part comprised of electromagnetic energy and thus enable us to experience God.

It is this INTENSE ELECTROMAGNETIC ENERGY WHICH MAKES THE SEXUAL EXPERIENCE SO EUPHORIC and sought after by so many people today, as unpopular or unlikely as this may seem for people with fundamentalist religious beliefs. The power and presence of this "sexual energy" is considerably diminished, however, when we do in fact allow our passions of just physical gratification from the sexual experience to rule over our lives. And, it is conversely augmented and lengthened when we realize that the most important and significant aspect of the sexual experience is manifested when we realize the central importance of the spiritual/God connection.

WHEN SEXUAL ENERGY IS CREATED IN ITS DIVINE ASPECT, TREMENDOUS AMOUNTS OF ENERGY FLOW THROUGH THE HEAD AND UP AND DOWN THE SPINAL COLUMN, CREATING AN INDESCRIBABE FEELING OF EUPHORIA. This energy produced is similar to a Kundalini Awakening!

If we are constantly seeking sexual gratification with the most voluptuous and/or perfect sexual partner in disregard to special spiritual aspects of sexual relations, the most important benefits of sex partially, if not completely, elude us. This is likewise the case when we concentrate more on sexual movements/positions and less/none on the energizing, balancing, healing aspects of the sexual energies which we experience, especially during orgasm. While it would be hard to deny there are physical pleasures related to orgasm, the profound spiritual states of being which allow us access to God through the electromagnetic energy generated, are vastly more significant and beneficial. This has been known and practiced in the East through such disciplines and Tantric Yoga and Taoism. All of these things are explained in more detail in Chapter Three of *A Map to Healing and Your Essential Divinity: The Physics of the Immortal 'Light Body' and The Creator's Template of Perfection for His Peoples,* by Dr. Newton.

Books which relate directly or indirectly to the God/sex relationship are: *Sexual Secrets: The Alchemy of Ecstasy,* by Nik Douglas & Penny Slinger; *The Tao of Sexology: The Book of Infinite Wisdom,* by Stephen T. Chang; *The Tao of the Loving Couple: True Liberation Through the Tao,* by

Jolan Chang; *The Eastern Way of Love: Tantric Sex & Erotic Mysticism*, by Kamela Devi; *The Taoist Secrets of Love: Cultivating Male Sexual Energy*, by Mantak Chia & Michaels Winn; and *Sex Psychic Energy*, by Betty Bethards.

There are also several sports which are extremely powerful and effective in creating or attracting the presence of God. One such sport is surfing. Experienced surfer's who are in the tube, with a wave barreling over their head, are very familiar with this unique encounter with God. There is no other activity which can duplicate this special experience, because you are entering an energy vortex where time is more or less suspended. Other sports are snow skiing and snowboarding. Experienced skiers/boarders know the euphoric feeling of almost floating down a hillside. This feeling may be replicated or even exceeded during skydiving and sky sailing. All of these sports allow the opportunity for profound experienced encounters with God because of a dimensional shift that is occurring in consciousness.

Next we will examine the uses of Energy Vortexes to magnify the presence of God in our lives, following these exercises.

EXERCISE _____

Perform either the Tai Chi Standing Meditation or The Do-In Standing Meditation or both. Feel how energized you are after only a short period of time. This is God's presence being more powerfully experienced in your life.

CHAPTER 9

Energy Vortexes—Extra High Concentrations Of God

Energy vortexes are in abundance all over the Earth. They are created when electromagnetic lines of energy, commonly called Leylines, cross each other from opposite directions and intersect. These lines crisscross all over the entire planet, but they do not always run exactly straight at all points in a north-south or east-west directions. Leylines are usually found in groups of three, five, seven, and fourteen. They can be detected with an electrometer, an aurameter, or dowsing rods. Dowsing rods are comprised of L-shape metal rods, usually from copper or brass, which rotate in a sleeve of similar metal or plastic. Sleeves are used to allow the rods to swing freely, so that they are in a state to be receptive to the electromagnetic energies. Crude dowsing rods can be made very simply from clothes hanger wire and paper or copper dowels. To construct your own dowsing rods, refer to the diagram at the end of the chapter.

Once you have these rods, you can detect Leylines and their vortexes (intersections). The benefit that these energy vortexes provide for us is that God's energy is concentrated at these points. Meditating in one of these vortexes enhances the meditational experience and makes our encounters with God even more meaningful because of the concentrated electromagnetism to which we are then subjected.

While these vortexes offer us a definite benefit, some people caution should not sleep in a leyline vortex or a set of leylines. This is because research in the Geopathic Sciences, most of it occurring in West Germany, has revealed a significantly higher incidence of cancer and other disorders related to sleeping in them. The author slept for several years under a pyramid with no adverse effects and actually had a significance increase in his psychic abilities occur. The pyramid itself creates an electromagnetic vortex, so possibly sleeping in a leyline vortex is not harmful!

Most people will be able to locate a vortex of at least a three Leyline Intersection close to where they live. These are the most common type. Spaced out at greater intervals are five Leyline vortexes and even more distanced are the seven and fourteen Leyline intersections. The Great Pyramid in Egypt is built on a fourteen Leyline vortex as is Stonehenge in England. The Washington Monument is located approximately two or three hundred yards from a seven Leyline vortex and was marked, if not discovered, by Thomas Jefferson. This is one reason there is "so much energy" in D.C. Also, Boynton Canyon and Bell Rock, in Sedona, Arizona, and Mt. Shasta, in California, have seven Leyline intersections, as does Lourdes, France. Such places as the Bermuda Triangle and Lake Erie also contain fourteen leyline vortexes, which is why so many unusual events transpire within their boundaries.

Not only is God's presence more intensified in these vortexes, they also TEND TO SYNCHRONIZE THE HEMISPHERES OF THE BRAIN which greatly increases our ability to sense God BECAUSE CONSCIOUSNESS HAS BEEN EXPANDED AND ENHANCED. From many experiences in various vortexes, the author personally knows how much easier God is to experience in these energy intersections! There is a "lightheaded" feeling and phenomena of electromagnetism that occurs, which often permeates the entire body. Sensations, similar to those of Tai Chi, may be experienced. The illustrations that follow show how to make dowsing rods from clothes hanger wire, and now, do a standard meditation or a Tai Chi "Standing Meditation" session. Note any and all sensations by which God may be "communicating" with you. Where the Leylines cross is the center of the energy vortex. Dowsing rods, when placed in the Leyline intersection will spin in a clockwise circular fashion in the Northern Hemisphere and vice-versa for the Southern Hemisphere. In these Leyline intersections, you will discover that the presence of God is significantly magnified!

Diagram:7

SIMPLE DOWSING ROD CONSTRUCTION

Take a wire hanger with a paper dowel on the bottom
part of the hanger.

wire hanger

paper dowel

Cut the paper dowel into 2 equal parts

½ OF WIRE HANGER BENT INTO "L" SHAPE

½ OF PAPER DOWEL

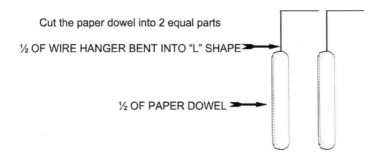

INSERT A WIRE "L" HALF INTO PAPER DOWEL HALF
NOW YOU HAVE THE REQUISITE 2 DOWSING RODS.
AFTER YOU REALIZE THIS REALLY IS USEFUL YOU CAN BUY BETTER CON-
STRUCTED DOWSING RODS.

EXERCISE _____

Now that you have made your own set of dowsing rods or purchased a professional type, try to find a set of energy lines or vortexes somewhere near your home. Begin your search by holding the rods so that they point forward, away from, and perpendicular to your body. Pick a direction, north to south or east to west and walk in a straight line. As you pass a Leyline, the rods will align themselves with the Leyline, at one point becoming parallel with it. As you pass over each line, the rods will swing forward again before crossing the next one. Count each line that you cross. You may need to correct your path in order to pass perpendicularly over the Leylines. Once you have determine the direction and number of Leylines in one direction, turn 90 degrees in either direction, following the Leyline path to determine if/where there is a set of crossing Leylines. It will probably take some time to "fine tune" the locations—be patient. It will be worth the effort, or so many students have told the author!

DOWSING FOR LEYLINES

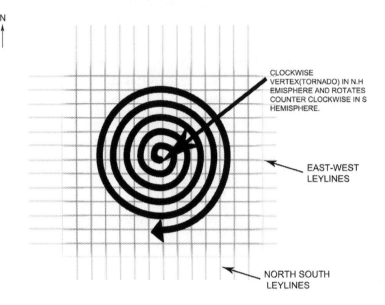

CLOCKWISE VERTEX(TORNADO) IN N.H EMISPHERE AND ROTATES COUNTER CLOCKWISE IN S HEMISPHERE.

EAST-WEST LEYLINES

NORTH SOUTH LEYLINES

DIAGRAM #7

SEARCHPATTERN: DOWSER SEARCHES FOR LEYLINES IN A N-S & E-W DIRECTION AS YOU ENCOUNTER A LEYLINE, THE DOWSING RODS WILL PUSH APART.WHEN YOU ENTER A VORTEX,THE RODS SPIN CLOCKWISE.

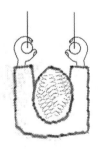

The human dowser holds the rods (not the dowel) parallel with the ground, arms outstretched and separated about shoulder width apart, hands facing each other but with the hand closed so that the dowsing rod can be grasped & operated.

TOP VIEW

A VORTEX OCCURS WHERE N-S & E-W LEYLINES INTERSECT. THE NATURE OF VORTEXES & LEYLINES IS E.M ENERGY/PRANA/CHI/LIFE FORCE.When Leylines are grouped (occur in multiples), they will be at least several feet apart. Also, they do not localize but rather circumnavigate the Earth

CHAPTER 10

Endorphins—The "Natural High" And A Pathway To God

We have already discussed the presence and function of endorphins somewhat in previous chapters. It has been found that these mind altering substances are released during the altered brain/consciousness levels of Alpha, Theta, and Delta. These three levels of consciousness are produced by meditation, mantras, postures and movements (including exercise and sports), toning, singing, music and sound, certain colors, and breathing techniques. They are also produced through the use of pyramids, gemstones, and polarized magnets which will be discussed in the following chapters. However, in this chapter we will investigate mental, visual, and sensory means of stimulating endorphins.

Endorphins are substances released by the brain during pleasurable experiences and sensations and memories of such. Endorphins are discussed in detail in *The Pleasure Connection,* by Beck and Beck and *The Complete Guide to Your Emotions and Your Health,* by Emrika Padus. Basically, what is important to know about these brain chemicals is that they can make us feel anywhere from good to blissful or euphoric, and detensify or eliminate pain in the body. When we are in this altered state of consciousness, we are much more likely to experience God via electromagnetism (tingling, etc.), light, sound, vibration, and warmth. These are means by which God transfers It's intelligence and love to us.

Beginning with mental methods of stimulating the release of endorphins, it is important to note just how powerfully our own thoughts and the words related to these thoughts are. This was graphically shown to the author by Serge King, a Hawaiian Huna (medicine man), through something as simple as muscle testing. You can duplicate this experience but you will need one other person to aid you. Extend your right arm straight out from your side and have another person attempt to push this arm down while you resist their efforts. Note how much your arm is depressed, and return your arm to its original position. Then say something derogatory about yourself such as "I am stupid and worthless", and repeat the arm straight out position with the same person pushing down again. For the author and everyone else he has ever tested, everybody has been considerably weaker than during the first test. When you are finished with the second test, repeat "Cancel, Cancel" out loud, as this will negate the derogatory statement about yourself. This can also be performed via Kinesiology "finger muscle testing", as is discussed in Chapter Four of Dr. Newton's, "A Map to Healing and Your Essential Divinity".

Now, return your arm to the rest position and say something derogatory about someone else. Repeat the arm test position again and you will be weaker than the first test and as weak or even weaker than the second test! Remember to repeat the phrase "Cancel, Cancel" again when you have completed your test. What does all of this reveal? Simply, that your thoughts and words can make you physically weaker and cause actual changes in your body and life. If you repeat tests number two and three but instead say something affirmative about yourself and someone else, you will not only be stronger than in tests number two and three, but also one. In conjunction with this, when you catch yourself saying something negative about yourself or another person, always say "Cancel, Cancel", as per the Silva Mind Control technique.

Now that it is apparent that we can create things in our life by our words, which are thoughts, let us consider what happens when we replay or re-visualize a pleasurable experience or sensation from our past. The most usual consequence of such an exercise is a happy feeling that comes over us, altered levels of brain functioning at the Alpha, Theta, or Delta levels, and the release of endorphins which will prolong all of the foregoing processes. Thus, *THINKING POSITIVE, SEEING POSITIVE, AND FEELING POSITIVE EQUALS THE CONDITIONS, namely, endorphins, FOR EXPERIENCING GOD CONSCIOUSNESS, i.e., intelligence and love.*

This equation is also relevant to fragrances. From the field of aromatherapy, we know that any fragrance which we consider enjoyable will create a positive mental and emotional outlook, release endorphins, and allow us to experience more Divinity. However, there are specific fragrances such as Sandalwood, Frankincense, Myrrh, Lotus, and Patchouli that will reliably enhance the endorphin/Divinity phenomenon. This has been known for thousands of years.

The equation also applies to laughter and humor. Not only do these two "tonics" relieve stress and negativity as well as full diaphragmatic breathing, they are exceptionally effective in stimulating endorphins. Enough cannot be said about the continual importance of humor and laughter in keeping us balanced, in a good mood, and thus more actually aligned with God we become! Also foods which we find pleasurable to eat will generally create the conditions for endorphin production. This effect can be negated by foods which contain toxic substances such as drugs, caffeine, sugar, and alcohol. All of these toxins will also deplete the electromagnetic or etheric force field (God) around the body. This negating effect also occurs with foods which are very fatty, acidic, and hard to digest. More information on this will be presented in Section Three.

While nicotine will produce the flow of endorphins, it is not recommended as an endorphin producer because of other detrimental side effects resulting from this drug. Also drugs, alcohol, and sugar, while originally creating experiences that closely replicate the effect and result of endorphins, after a short period of usage they cannot reproduce the quasi-duplicate conditions. And they actually suppress the production of endorphins for many months after their usage has been terminated!

Thus, DRUGS, ALCOHOL AND SUGAR EQUAL NO ENDORPHINS AND A SUPRRESION OF GOD CONSCIOUSNESS, *over the long run,* although we "feel good" when we first use these substances. So this could be summed up in the following phrase: The more you "use", the more you need, the more you use, the more you lose! This is explained in detail in Dr. Newton's, "A Map to Healing and Your Essential Divinity Through Theta Consciousness".

EXERCISE

Try visualizing something pleasurable from your past or create a fantasy experience you would like to experience. Be as vivid and realistic and detailed as possible. After a few minutes do you feel better? If so, you have triggered endorphins and expanded God Consciousness!

CHAPTER 11

Using Nature To Invoke God's Power And Presence

The Native American Indian teachings and many of the world's ancient spiritual traditions indicate that man is dependent on nature not only for sustenance of the body but also for emotional and spiritual balance. It is the emotional and spiritual balance that are so critically important for us if we are to have success in feeling God's power and presence.

How can the plant, mineral, and animal kingdoms help us to create emotional and spiritual balance? Simply put, they are able to absorb or transmute our lower emotions (depression, anger, fear, and resentment) so that we can elevate our consciousness to the higher emotions (joy, humor, laughter). How this absorption or transmutation of emotions occurs is not specifically known at this time. However, it is known that these three kingdoms are here in order to aid man in evolving to higher levels of consciousness and divinity.

We know from Peter Tompkins book, *The Secret Life of Plants,* trees and plants do in fact react to our emotions, thus they must have some sort of intelligence or consciousness. We further know that there are "spirits" which inhabit mature trees, a concept which is understood by almost every primitive culture but not today. Thus the practice of hugging a tree does in fact benefit us as many people who have tried this can testify. From personal experience, Doc can attest to the tremendous energy transference which can take place while hugging a mature tree, especially old ones such as the giant redwoods or old oak trees.

Relating an experience of hugging a tree can never compare with actually doing it yourself. However, the author experiences a soothing of emotional trauma and a feeling euphoria, akin to a state of divinity, as well as transference of calming energy. He has found that in order to obtain the greatest benefit, you must be relaxed and surrender to the consciousness of the tree. The author has also found similar benefits just by walking through a forest in a leisurely manner. Many hikers and riders are familiar with the soothing and uplifting feeling that emanates from the forest and the outdoors in general.

Even with the mineral kingdom, there can be beneficial encounters for human beings. In *Kinship With all Life,* there is revealed an experience between a person and a large boulder in which the person could actually communicate with the intelligence or consciousness residing therein. An attempt to "tune in" into the consciousness of a boulder usually takes time and is best accomplished by lying down next to, or sitting on the boulder. It has been speculated that the stability and duration of time that such mineral specimens have existed accounts for their ability to soothe and uplift us. Again, from personal experience, the author has found great comfort and peace from attempting similar experiences with boulders!

Also such vast expanses as deserts, which are bountifully supplied with almost all minerals and rocks, can have a dramatically soothing and uplifting experience on humans. This may sound rather strange by those people who feel they need to be surrounded by lush greenery to be serene. However, it simply requires the ability to perceive and appreciate the subtle aspects of nature, and this will often allow a great calm to come over us even while in a desert environment, which contains subtle forms (plants) of green.

With regards to the sea, there are very few people who do not enjoy being by or in an ocean environment. Besides the benefit of the uplifting effect of negative ions, there is the overall ability of the oceans to cleanse, balance and transmute any traumatic emotions which we may be carrying with us. Edgar Cayce, in his psychic readings related the emotional benefits found by interacting with the ocean.

Finally, many people will acknowledge the soothing feelings they experience with domesticated animals such as cats, dogs, horses, etc. Again, these have been greatly detailed in *Kinship With All Life*. These experiences can also extend to the wilder forms of the animal kingdom such as deer, rabbits, squirrels, and birds. Especially in the case of birds we can learn symbolically how to transcend our troubles and worries by simply flying or lifting ourselves above them. And with deer, we can marvel at how well they can jump over their obstacles and problems.

In the Native American teachings, it is told that we can learn how to understand and cope with life on earth from observation and respect of nature. Even people living in the country, but especially those people living in the city, could be well advised to acquaint or reacquaint themselves with nature. When we can open our minds to the fact that something which we have considered an inferior aspect of creation exerts a calming effect on us, a new avenue can be opened to experience God. Thus the author encourages all people seeking God to spend as much time as possible in and around the forests, mountains, deserts, oceans, and gardens. If you try this you will more than likely enjoy yourself! Let us next explore pyramid energies in the next chapter.

EXERCISE

By yourself or with similar minded individuals, allow yourself to experience the soothing and uplifting aspects of nature by hugging a mature tree and then do the same thing with a large boulder. Also, take time to observe birds and how they can fly above their troubles on the earth. If you can observe deer at anytime, notice how they leap over or around almost any obstacle. These exercises will be more dramatically beneficial for you if done during a period of emotional trauma or general dissatisfaction with life or specific problems. Note your initial experiences and repeat the exercises on a regular basis. You should see yourself becoming more emotionally balanced and spiritually uplifted after a period of time has passed by practicing these exercises regularly!

CHAPTER 12

Pyramid Energies

O NE OF THE MOST POWERFUL DEVICES TO ATTRACT "LIFE FORCE", or the "God Energies", IS THE PYRAMID. Despite the fact that there has been great skepticism on the value and effectiveness of the pyramid form, it is, nevertheless, an ARCHETYPE/ TEMPLATE upon which BASIC CREATION is BASED, from the atomic level on one end of the continuum to the extraterrestrial on the other extreme. Let us first examine the subatomic/atomic and sub-molecular/molecular levels.

Through the miracle of the Helium ion (electron) microscope, Ervin W. Mueller has photographed **PLATINUN CRYSTALS**, and what is **REVEALED IS A MATRIX OF INTERLOCKING TRIANGLES/PYRAMIDS** (refer to picture of this in "A Map to Healing and Your Essential Divinity', in Chapter Five, by Dr, Newton). Also, in *The Death of Ignorance,* Dr. Fred Bell's research revealed that silver has a tetrahedral pyramid shape and gold has an octahedral pyramid shape. Furthermore, we know that as blood crystallizes, it assumes pyramid shapes. Also, the hydrogen atom, probably our cleanest power source of energy, forms a *Star of David,* which is the result of two overlapping pyramids. As Bruce Cathie points out in *The Bridge to Infinity,* there are harmonic calculations associated with the pyramid which are related to the harmonics of the atom. Thus we have CLEAR EVIDENCE THAT THE PYRAMID SHAPE IS A VITAL FORM ON THE ATOMIC LEVEL AND FOR "PHYSICAL" LIFE TO EXIST and is necessary for the existence of our most valuable metals used on Earth.

Additionally, we know from the research by Valery P. Kondratov. in her treatise, *The Lightning From Pyramids,* that **there are strong characteristics of electricity which emanate from the pyramid form**. This can be sensed at the apex of a pyramid, when you are standing upon it. Certainly, for Dr. Newton, the performance of the Tai Chi "Standing Meditation was more energizing while he was standing atop the "Great Pyramid" in Egypt. The electrical resonance field generated from pyramids is 11 GHz, which just happens to be the same frequency resonation as the mineral, Quartz. Dr. Newton would not be surprised if many individual atoms resonated at this frequency likewise. Irrespective of this, there is a mutual resonance amplification when Quartz and pyramids are used conjunctively. Also these same resonance fields should exist between these things and the human body, since it is partially comprised of the Silicon Dioxide which is contained in Quartz.

On an architectural level, we not only have physical evidence of pyramids in Egypt and Mexico, we also know that there are pyramids in China that go back at least 5000 years in recorded history and probably 12000 years and even more. We have pictures of such a pyramid, at Sensei, in Cathie's *Bridge to Infinity.* There is also evidence that there may indeed be pyramids in the Himalayas and Peru also.

Furthermore, the obelisk form, which still exists today in Egypt, is an archetype which is identified with the Freemasons, and in the United States, the Washington Monument is thought to be the most powerful landmark in Washington, D.C. Additionally, spires, which are a modified pyramid form, are prominently displayed on famous cathedrals, temples, and churches all over the world. The tepee shape of the American Indian tents is also a pyramid form. These pyramid qualities are also contained within such buildings as the Empire State Building in New York, and the Trans America Building in San Francisco, California.

As Dr. Newton explains in his book, *A Map to Healing and Your Essential Divinity,* the triangle is the basis of our modern engineering, especially in bridges. **Is it just coincidental that this is a replication of the atomic level?** More than likely, it indicates that the Creator knows how to construct "strong forms" and somehow, humans learned how to replicate this!

On another level, we know that when objects with sharp edges, such as knives or razor blades, are placed under a pyramid, they become re-sharpened. We also know that pyramid energies act as a preservative on many foodstuffs. And, we know that when gemstones are placed under a pyramid, especially piezoelectric minerals such as quartz, topaz, and tourmaline, they become optically clearer and assume more sparkle and radiance. We further know that pyramids can re-energize dormant seeds and speed their germination,

At the extraterrestrial level, the pyramid form is well represented on the planet Mars. In *The Monuments of Mars,* by Richard Hoagland, there are photos from the Mariner 9 Mission which clearly reveal three different types of pyramids, three, four, and five sided forms. This indicates that not only pyramids exist on another planet, but so did other civilization or civilizations.

At the level of "outer space", the dying star, *MWC 922,* has the shape of an Octahedron. It is virtually **impossible to state, without substantial ignorance, that the pyramid form is a random or chaotic occurrence within creation. Rather, a synchronistic pattern of pyramidal shapes reveals itself from all levels, from the sub-atomic to the macro-cosmic!!!!** There is a great picture of *MWC 922* in Valery P. Kondratov's, *Geometry of a Uniform Field,* which can be internet accessed.

Aside from any technical aspects related to pyramids, WHAT MAKES PYRAMIDS VALUABLE is that they PROFOUNDLY AID IS IN

EXPERIENCING GOD! According to Manly P. Hall, in *The Secret Teachings of All Ages,* originally the word **pyramid** came from the word **fire.** Cathie, in *The Bridge to Infinity,* elaborates on this even more by revealing that *pyramid* means *fire in the middle.* However, Cathie further adds that the actual translation of this should be **"the lights"**. Pyramid then, would be translated in the Greek or Semitic languages meaning **"the lights" or "light measures"**. This would thus indicate that the people of these languages knew of the electrical nature of pyramids!

But how do these esoteric concepts relate actually to God? The answer to this is obvious to any student of the ancient religious traditions including Judaism and Christianity since the symbols of fire and light have been used since the beginning of recorded history and religion to denote the presence of God. Has not God been revealed as appearing in a *burning bush* or as an *intensely blinding light?* In some mysterious manner then, God is captured or powerfully contained within the pyramid form and/or functions more powerfully therein!

The pyramid form is similar in function to an antenna. It can be classified as a cosmic or heavenly antenna whereby we can attune to, and accept the presence and power of God. Marshall McLuhan concluded after his extensive research, that a pyramid is a resonating chamber akin to a brass musical instrument or stereo speaker enclosure. We can also surmise that the pyramid must be an intense electromagnetic generator since the attempt to photograph the Great Pyramid with X-rays was interfered with by some mysterious force emanating there from. As has been mentioned many times previously, electromagnetism is an aspect of God. Therefore, GOD POWERFLLY MANIFESTS ITSELF IN THE PYRAMID FORM!

Certainly, the Egyptians were aware of the Life Force Energies of God contained within the pyramid shape. Such energies are indicated from the photos generated by Kirilian photography. After being subjected to pyramid energies, the etheric or electromagnetic field around the physical body or a plant is at least **doubled** for a significant duration following exposure. This is clearly presented by the pictures in *Pyramid Power,* by G. Patrick Flanagan. As Bruce Cathie states in his book, the

PYRAMID IS A GENERATOR WHICH COLLECTS INTENSE ELECTROMAGNETISM!

Dr. Fred Bell has done other research contained in *The Death of Ignorance,* showing that a **pyramid either attracts or generates negative ions in significant concentrations,** beyond that occurring naturally, as was stated several paragraphs earlier. We know from Dr. Bell's work and that of Dr. Donsbach in *Negative Ions,* that these electromagnetic charges create better, more positive mental and emotional states of consciousness. Certainly these states of higher consciousness allow us to be more receptive to God! WE ALSO KNOW THAT NEGATIVE IONS HELP TO BUILD NERVE, CELL, AND BRAIN TISSUES and HELP HEAL SICKNESS AND DISEASE. This enhanced state of physical well being is also another aid in building our receptiveness to God!

Many people, including the author, have had extremely powerful electromagnetic interchanges with God inside the Great Pyramid in Giza, Egypt. These pyramid experiences often involve vastly altered states of consciousness at the level of **Theta or Delta brainwaves/ consciousness. These levels of consciousness seem to be a direct pathway to God** and divine inspiration. This might have been one of the motivations behind John Lily's brain/mind research.

These pyramid experiences can often be duplicated using scale versions of the Great Pyramid. Scale models can be as small as an eight inch base, with larger models up to ten feet or more, and are often open sided (holographic representations). By placing your head or heart under the apex (point) of the pyramid, the altered brainwaves already referred to are produced, at least at the Alpha level. Prayer and meditation are greatly facilitated by this action also. Attention and focus are accentuated by the pyramid form, as are desire and intent. When brainwaves are measured on an EEG machine, after exposure to pyramid energies they exhibit the characteristics of Alpha/Theta, and in some cases, Delta levels of consciousness.

When pyramids are constructed from the mineral, Quartz, and other piezoelectric stones such as topaz or tourmaline, and various metals, **their effectiveness in collecting or generating and dispensing the electrical energies of God is significantly magnified because of their sympathetic resonance**s, as illustrated in the research of Valery P. Kondratov, mentioned earlier in this chapter. Although there is a pervasive belief that pyramids constructed from copper are vastly superior to all others, Dr. Bell discovered that pyramids made with gold and/or titanium are omnidirectional, and therefore are the most powerful attractants of God. Thus, to have a powerful effect in magnifying God's presence, the gold plated pyramids do not need to be oriented to magnetic north as do the copper and other types. He further discovered that by applying the research of Wilheim Reich, using two or more different metals reproduced the **Orgone effect,** resulting from the **combining of dissimilar materials** (a mixture of different things).

The *Orgone Effect*, in this case, is the creation of more energy from combining various materials which exceeds the sum total of the various material when measured separately. The resulting pyramid from the combination of diverse metals is significantly more attractive to God's Life Force energies. When we use the north (negative charge) side of magnets on the apex and in the corners of the pyramid, the electromagnetic energies will be considerably magnified, because a state of relaxation occurs that allows us to access God. with less interference. However, do not attempt to use magnets with a pyramid until you have read the next chapter on magnets because it is essential that they be used in a specific manner for user safety.

Place polarized disc magnets in all corners, with South Pole (positive charge) taped to pyramid, and North Pole (or negative charge) facing inward. On the apex (top), tape a South Pole (positive charge) of the magnet taped to the pyramid and North Pole (negative charge) facing downward. NEVER REVERSE THESE POLARITIES UNLESS YOU HAVE CONSULTED WITH AN EXPERT IN MAGNETIC HEALING!

Begin by using magnets in the 600-1200 gauss range, and when you are accustomed to those, increase the strength to 1200-2800 gauss range, gradually. Having a magnometer, which is an instrument that indicates the "plus and negative" charges of a magnet, makes the job of ascertaining magnet polarity immensely easier and almost a necessity!

PLACEMENT OF MAGNETS & CRYSTALS ON A PYRAMID

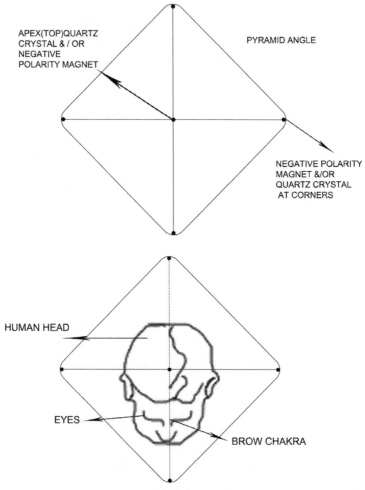

ALIGN A PYRAMID CORNER BETWEEN THE EYES SO THAT IT ALIGNS WITH BROW (FOREHEAD) CHAKRA.THE APEX ALIGNS WITH THE TOP OF THE HEAD.

We now have other powerful pyramid archetypes by which to attract and experience God, specifically three and five sided pyramids as depicted in Richard Hoagland's, *The Monuments of Mars*. Dr. Hurtak reveals in *The Keys of Enoch,* that the mere visualizing of a pyramid over your head will more fully infuse our bodies with electromagnetic energies! It will also raise your bodily vibration to a more sympathetic level compatible with the Adam Kadmon archetype, i.e., the perfect man created in the image and likeness of God. Hence, we have another simple way to "tune in" to God. As Bruce Cathie, Edgar Cayce, Dr. Bell, Dr. Hurtak, Rev. Chuck Schwartz, Gandalph Slick, Doug Benjamin and a multitude of other writers and researchers have expressed, in contradiction to most Egyptologists, the pyramid was not built for the dead, but rather the living in order to expand their minds and consciousness of God. The "Great Pyramid" may have also been used as a power source to run electrical devices as per Christopher Dunn's book, *Giza Power Plant"* and Gerry E. Bayless' website, *Current Power Generation* or for nuclear energy as per Keith Hunter's website, *Nuclear Pyramid.com*.

We know from Gandalph Slick's, *The Rosey Tablet,* that THE HARMONICS OF THE GREAT PYRAMID RESONATE WITH THE HUMAN HEART. Whether the tetrahedron shape of the three sided pyramid is more powerful for the new age, as Dr. Hurtak claims, is uncertain at this time. From the author's experiences and that of other pyramidologist's he has consulted with, the quadrahedron (four sided pyramid) still seems to be a very powerful shape at this time. Whether this will change, possibly even to the five sided pyramid as found on Mars, is unknown with any certainty at the present time.

There is a pyramid medallion, developed by Dr. Bell, known as the *Nuclear Receptor.* This medallion allows the wearer to receive the continual benefit of the Life Force God Energies of the pyramid without having to subject oneself to possible ridicule in public by wearing a scale model pyramid on the head. The *Nuclear Receptor is* worn over the heart and is comprised of 144 very small pyramids modeled according to the Great Pyramid archetypal form. (Twelve times twelve equals 144, and is considered a sacred number of creation). The receptor also incorporates the *Solar Cross* of the Archangel Michael, also known as Ra, Ra Ta, Helios, Apollo, Misol Ha, Sol, Hod, and Vishnu, among others. The Catholic Church has acknowledged Michael as the *Angel of Protection* and *The Keys of Enoch* has recognized Michael as the dispenser of *Light* into our Solar System.

There is an incredible painting and print by Nanette M.A. Crist of the Archangel Michael, in which Michael himself is wearing a medallion which closely resembles the *Nuclear Receptor.* The amazing aspect of this coincidence is that Nan Crist had never seen a *Nuclear Receptor* until long after her painting was completed. The evidence would tend to indicate then, that the *Nuclear Receptor is* a powerful device by which to attract the God Energies for more than one reason of the pyramids shapes.

When pyramids are connected into interlocking grid works and matrixes such as those created by Dr. Bell at Pyradyne, or those created by Metaforms, the pyramid electromagnetic devices by which we can invoke the presence of God. The author knows from personal research and experience, that Dr. Bell's **Irradiator** and **Orb Matrixes** can generate and radiate the God energies in an extremely concentrated form.

Finally, from *The Rosey Tablet,* by Gandalph Slick, we have revealed how the harmonics of the pyramid shapes can activate and effectuate healing, according to pyramid angle, of various body organs and acupuncture points and meridians. This is explained in the following chart on the next page:

PYRAMID HARMONICS AND THEIR RELATIONSHIP TO NOTES, ORGANS AND ACCUPUNTURE POINTS:

PRYAMID ANGLE	SCALE NOTE	BODY ORGAN	ACCUPTR. POINT
59 degrees	A	Hindbrain	Triple Warmer
58 degrees	A	Midbrain	Triple Warmer
57 degrees	G	Stomach	
56 degrees	A		Triple Warmer
55 degrees	A	Forebrain	Triple Warmer
54 degrees	F	Small Intestine	
53 degrees	F#	Bladder	
52 degrees	C	Heart	Central/ Governing Meridians
51 degrees	E	Lung	
50 degrees	G#	Large Intestine	
49 degrees	C#	Kidney	
48 degrees	D	Pericardium	
47 degrees	B	Gall Bladder	
46 degrees	A#	Spleen	
45 Degrees	D#	Liver	

For the purpose of this book, pyramids constructed at the fifty two degree angle, activates the Heart. At fifty five, fifty eight, and fifty nine degrees, a pyramid stimulates various portions of the Brain, and will enable us to receive the energies of God more completely at these pyramid angles!.

In the next chapter we will examine the use of polarized magnets to catalyze the Life Force God Energies.

EXERCISE _____

To begin a meditation session, visualize a pyramid placed over your head. Do you experience tingling, chills, warmth, or vibration in your head, heart, hands, or spinal column? Are you better able to receive any *messages* from God?

EXERCISE _____

With a pyramid which you can either put on your head or sit under, experience the pyramid energies and note any sensations as listed in the exercise above. Then, use the pyramid to facilitate a meditation session. Be aware of anything that might happen. Be sure that you are under the apex of the pyramid. Experiment with your pyramid in a subsequent meditation session by hanging a Quartz or Tourmaline point or rod from the apex and also try taping or wiring some crystals midway on the pyramid sides and corners. Do the same thing with north polarized magnets and note any and all things that transpire (North polarized magnets will be discussed in the next chapter). Are you able to achieve deeper levels of meditation? Do you feel more connected with God's presence?. Can you literally feel God coursing throughout your body?

CHAPTER 13

Using Magnets To Harness God's Energy

For most people, their experience with magnets involves *party tricks* or simple science demonstrations. The use of magnets for healing people and animals is gaining gradual acceptance in the United States. However, polarized healing magnets have been used in Japan for over thirty years and their effectiveness is truly amazing on a wide array of sickness and disease. The problem with magnets in the U.S. is that they must be sold for *research only,* and not specifically for healing. Nevertheless, they are available from several U.S. suppliers.

ANY AND ALL PEOPLE WHO USE MAGNETS WITHOUT THE APPROPRIATE POLARITY MUST ASSUME RESPONSIBILITY FOR ANY AND ALL DAMAGE TO THEIR BODIES, WHICH MIGHT ENSUE, including magnifying an infectious condition. It is the negative charge energies which relax the body and allow us to more profoundly experience GOD!

Before using any magnets, be certain they are charge identified and that you know the gauss strength. (The gauss is the unit of measure for magnet intensity). Although the gauss strength is not imprinted into the magnets, the negative polarity is sometimes identified by a dot of paint or painted green. The positive polarity is sometimes identified with red paint, or no marking at all if the negative polarity is already marked. Whereas the negative pole of the magnet induces relaxation and eliminates pain, the south pole of the magnet is highly energizing and increases pain but can also loosen "knotted" muscles and stimulate acupuncture points and speed the healing of bone fractures, provided there is no infection in the area treated.

Our goal in using magnets is to create a deeper relaxation and to charge the body with God's the magnet will *charge* the body much more rapidly with electromagnetic energies. So much so, it is recommended that the positive polarity be employed for only thirty to sixty seconds on the body, unless you are an experienced "Magnetic Healing" practitioner. It is considerably safer to use the negative pole, which can achieve the same results in anywhere from five to fifteen minutes. This will also **slow down brainwaves so that the mind/consciousness functions in the Alpha-Theta range or even upper Delta**, the three brain levels of God consciousness.

The magnets easiest to use are small disc magnets, which are pole identified and in the 900 to 2400 gauss range. They vary in size from about 1/8th to 1/2 inch in diameter, are thin like a wafer, and are made from ceramic, samarium cobalt, or neodymium. Some suppliers of these magnets are listed in the back of this book. IT WILL BE RE-EMPHASIZED THAT ANYONE WHO EXPERIEMENTS WITH THESE MAGNETS MUST ASSUME ALL REPONSIBILITY FOR THE CONSEQUENCES OF THEIR USE, AS MISUSE COULD CAUSE PAIN AND DAMAGE TO YOUR BODY!!!!

Besides the electromagnetic charging of the body and the altered states of brain functioning/consciousness, magnets may also enhance the negative ion effect around people, similar in effect to that of a pyramid. However, research to verify such claims needs to be undertaken first. Regardless of this negative ion effect, polarized magnets are powerful generators of God's presence similar to a pyramid in regard to the other aspects discussed. **Magnets merit use when done within the prescribed parameters discussed in this chapter!**

By placing the negative side/polarity of the magnet on the crown Chakra (middle, top of the head), you are using polarized magnets to charge the body with God's electromagnetic energies, by putting the body in a stronger state of relaxation. Begin with using magnets in the 900 to 1200 gauss strength range and build up to the 2000 to 2400 gauss range. If you want a **more dramatic charging effect on the body, you could place the negativity polarity of magnets placed simultaneously on each of the seven major Chakra** (refer to previous Chakra chart) while lying down! You could even add magnets to the minor Chakras to increase the effect. These magnets can be easily taped to the body.

To entrain brain levels of God consciousness (Alpha, Theta, Delta), placing a magnet on the crown Chakra and placing or taping a magnet on the brow Chakra, will activate the pituitary and pineal glands which help facilitate this process. There are also magnetic necklaces and bracelets which can be worn on the body continuously which will also help to attract and make you more receptive to God's energies.

Magnetic pads are the use of magnets on a larger scale, integrated into a grid work. The first modern magnetic pads came from Japan, consisting of a thin mattress embedded with 600 to 900 gauss strength magnets spaced throughout, on which you recline. Recently, many improvements have increased the benefits and effects of magnetic pads. One of these *pads,* created by Stephen Olender and called the "Crystal Magnetic Energy Balancing Port", contains many north polarized magnets integrated with quartz crystals and a modified Tesla Coil. Because the "Port" is energized by a power source, the effects generated can result in very euphoric encounters with God.

Not quite as dramatic as Stephen Olender's "Port" but still very energizing, is the "Bio-Magnetic Energizer", by Metaforms. It consists of magnets and crystals combined with a copper grid work and layers of different fabrics to create an Orgone Effect. The author has synthesized the best of Olender's "Energy Port" and the Metaforms "Energizer" into a creation, "The Electromagnetic Energizer", which not only contains crystals and magnets, but other gemstones as well. The author uses higher gauss strength magnets, employ a combination of fabrics, and have added a multi-metal grid work instead of just copper. As an option, this pad can also be connected to an external power source.

However, it has been realized that the power source is not necessary except for those people who wish to experience the effects of this pad at an extremely intense level. Dr. Newton can highly recommend all three of these newer magnetic pads as well as the older Japanese magnetic pads. The relaxation alone which is created, induces a dramatic benefit that ALLOWS THE USER TO RELAX INTO THEIR INHERENT EXISTING DIVINITY and all the benefits that accrue there from! THOSE PEOPLE WHO CANNOT EXERCISE CAUTION AND FOLLOW THE INSTRUCTIONS IN THIS CHAPTER, REGARDING THE USE OF INDIVIDUAL MAGNETS, SHOULD NOT USE THEM. If, however, "Nikken" bi-polar magnets are used, the above cautions do not apply!

The user of these magnetic pads can feel the electromagnetic presence of God to charging into the body after about five to fifteen minutes use. Furthermore, the entrained brain levels, from Alpha through Delta, which are effectuated, dramatically increase your ability to pray and meditate as well as increase the duration of these important activities. An often occurring phenomena related to these magnetic pads, is that you can easily learn to astral project out of your body, sometimes even on the atomic or subatomic level. This experience is a journey through a magnificent level of God's creation which can easily rival, if not surpass, the Aurora Borealis." "TRAVELING THROUGH THIS MICROCOSMIC/ATOMIC LEVEL OF CREATION CAN ALSO BE DISORIENTING AS WELL AS ASTONISHINLY BEAUTIFUL. This is similar to taking a "trip" on LSD, with similar effects related thereto!!!!

Although it has not yet been mentioned, the various magnets and magnetic devices will also aid in building the body's immune system. They are invaluable in healing sickness and disease even though no specific claims can be made of this according to FDA regulations.

These aspects will be discussed more in depth the later in the chapter on *Keeping the Body Healthy.*

The *Magnetic Hammer is* a rubber hammer embedded with a 1500 gauss strength magnet. It is made in Japan and is intended to eliminate aches and pains from the body as well as to stimulate acupuncture and acupressure points. It us used by tapping it on the body, generating a percussive action. However, it can just as easily be used in a rapid tapping motion to stimulate the spiritual Chakras such as the crown and brow energy centers.

The last magnetic device which will be discussed is the *Magnetic Polarizer,* which is a large electromagnet that works in the same manner as other magnets. The gauss strength is not rated on these devices, but they emit a powerful electromagnetic force field. You can generate either North or South pole magnetic energies simply by flipping a toggle switch. If the *Magnetic Polarizer* is hung under the apex of a large holographic pyramid, the energy created can be very blissful!

When the polarized disc magnets are used in the corners and apex of a pyramid, they will substantially increase the electromagnetic force field generated by the pyramid. You may want to start experimenting with the 900 gauss magnets in such an application and work your way up to the 2800 gauss. Use and apply these magnetic as was discussed earlier in the chapter or use "Nikken" bipolar magnets.

As was stated in the previous chapter, combining these two modalities, even though they are compatible, is a little too intense for some people. However, those people who are determined to experience God at its fullest potential, might find that the combination of pyramids and magnets to be a blissfully intense experiential encounter with God. But, in whatever application described in this chapter you choose to use these magnets or magnetic devices, they can be a direct aid in your quest in actually experiencing God!

In the next chapter we will look at other devices that entrain the brain into levels of God consciousness.

EXERCISE

In light of the precautions and disclaimers given, unless you use "Nikken" bi-polar magnets, purchase some polarized magnets and position them on your chakras, especially the crown and brow areas. Does your body feel energized? Do you feel different sensations in your head or an expansive feeling? Please make sure you are using the North (negative) Pole against the body? IMMEDIATELY DISCONTINUE USAGE OF THE MAGNETS IF YOU EXPERIENCE ANY DISCOMFORT OR PAIN, **SINCE YOU ARE MOST LIKELY USING THE WRONG POLARITY OF THE MAGNET**! Substitute "Nikken" bi-polar magnets for polarized magnets in this situation!

CHAPTER 14

Brain Entrainment Devices Which Create Levels Of God Consciousness

MANY OF US HAVE SEARCHED MUCH OF OUR LIVES "LOOKING" FOR GOD BUT WE ARE NOT PROPERLY PREPARED OR "EQUIPED" FOR THIS UNDERTAKING. Our BRAIN-COMPUTER, when it is PROPERLY ENTRAINED at the LEVELS of ALPHA, THETA, and Delta, BECOMES AN ANTENNA which is in a RECEPTIVE MODE TO EXPERIENCE the PRESENCE OF GOD! There is a guarantee that this will occur when combined with the intent to contact God, then a certainty of an encounter with God increases. Certainly prayer, and especially meditation, can produce these entrained states of God consciousness. But, many people have difficulty reaching these states of altered consciousness. We have already discussed how this can be done as a by-product of various practices and devices. However, we have not discussed devices which are specifically devoted to only creating the brain levels that can lead to cosmic or God consciousness.

There are devices today which create electronic pulsations that are induced into the body, can specifically create entrained levels of brain functioning. These devices often have incorporated into them various types of electromagnetic energy and/or audible sounds that can create these same brain levels with binaural beats. And most recently, they have incorporated the concept of using the stroboscopic effect to create a process called retina reversal, which takes place in the eye and the brain and produces brain entrainment.

While the author has personally found these devices useful in making his brain-computer more receptive to God's presence, he feels that generally they are overpriced in relation to the components they contain and their reliability over a period of time. Lor'D Industries, sells their "Alpha-Pacer" series of brain entrainment devices as does Lindemann Laboratories with their "Bio-Pacer" units. Also, there is the "Alpha Pacer II", the "Beck Brain Device", also known as the "Brain Tuner" and the "MC1-4" units. Additionally, there is "Hemi Synch" with the "D.A.V.I.D. 1" brain entraining device. This is not a complete list, but it is important to experience as many of these devices as possible before purchasing a specific one. Also, beware of their limitations and reliability. Also this is discussed more in Dr. Newton's, *A Map to Healing and Your Essential Divinity* regarding a device from *MIND TECH*.

Another useful, reliable, but expensive device, is the "See Chamber" by Reflections. This is a small chamber which is completely mirrored that you sit within. It creates over three hundred reflections of yourself and this phenomena creates **retina reversal** within the eye and brain that leads to the Alpha/Theta/Delta levels of brain functioning. The chamber is wired so that you can connect a sound system for music to enhance the retina reversal process. It is easy to achieve a euphoric sense of consciousness in these chambers that can lead to powerfully blissful experiences with God. Recently, strobe lights have been added to a device like this that intensifies the experience even more.

Also, a very effective device that allows us to more fully realize the presence of God is the flotation/sensory deprivation tank. This is a tank a little larger than the body, filled with salt water, with a light, and sound proof top. Users of this device float in the tank on their backs, and experience life without any distractions, as all the "chitter chatter" of life melts away and we become more aware of our Divinity! There are centers which rent time for using the sensory deprivation tanks. It is important to note that these devices and machines cannot do or produce anything that you cannot do by self induced means or techniques. Many people have found however, that these devices induce levels of God consciousness that they have never before experienced. For some people they will bring first encounters with God and thus will bring the long awaited breakthroughs. For other people their existing relationship with God is further deepened.

EXERCISE

Should you decide to purchase one of the devices discussed, follow the directions as indicated and note your first experiences. Maintain a record, and see if they change over a period of usage. Do you feel more relaxed? Are you in a better mood? Do you feel more at one with God? Are you receiving bio-feedback of this? Notice if you react to stress more effectively. Are your spiritual desires intensified?

CHAPTER 15

The Benefit Of Negative Ions In Our Quest For God

Negative ions are necessary for us to lead healthful, fruitful, and spiritual lives. It is not that positive ions are *bad,* but when negative ions diminish from the optimal ratio of twelve positive ions to ten negative ions, it seems to be harder function at our full potential either on the physical or spiritual levels. Although there is little information published in regard to negative ions, Dr. Donsbach's book, *Negative Ions,* and Dr. Bell's, *The Death of Ignorance,* includes a comprehensive overview of the importance of these electronically charged particles.

While many people know that negative ions create enhanced emotional moods for humans, very few are aware that a deficiency of negative ions conversely causes people to be more irritable, nervous, and possibly violent. These emotional states create "wedges" between us and God, lessening our experiencing of the God Energies. "Chinook" or "Santa Ana" winds (of the hot and dry type) and the time just before a rainstorm, are examples of negative ion depleted situations which naturally occur and help to create serontin in the body. It is the serontin which causes the negative attributes just ascribed to the deficiency of negative ions and surplus of positive ions.

There are even indications that solar magnetic storms associated with sunspots can significantly deplete negative ions. Even worse than these naturally occurring situations, are the artificially created situations leading to negative ion impoverished conditions. These artificial forces include air pollution and electrical wave pollution comprised of extra low frequency waves (ELF), high voltage electrical transmissions, household and business electrical wiring systems, radar, microwave transmission, radio, and television.

Negative ions may possibly be even of greater importance in their role of rebuilding nerve, cell, and brain tissues, as discovered by Dr. Bell. And, Dr. Donsbach relates how not only sickness and disease are cured through negative ion therapy, but also how people's energy levels increase after exposure to a concentrated dose of negative ions. Fortunately for us, there are many naturally occurring situations where negative ions are present in abundance. These situations of natural ion generation occur anywhere there is crashing, falling, or running water. Thus, negative ions will always be found in abundance at the beach, by rivers, and next to waterfalls. Negative ions are also plentiful when you are taking a shower. They can be artificially created by negative ion devices, even including devices made for the car environment by negative ion generators.

Also, such things as pyramids and piezoelectric minerals (the quartzes, topazes, and tourmalines) either generate or attract negative ions. These things all work well in an interior environment. Waterfalls and fountains can be built in the outdoor or indoor environment with circulating pool pumps. Such things will fill the air with beneficial negative ions around houses and businesses!

So how, you might ask, does all this relate to attracting the presence of God in our lives? Simply put, IF WE FEEL BETTER, WE PERFORM BETTER, PHYSICALLY, EMOTIONALLY, MENTALLY AND SPIRIUALLY. This is basically an unarguable statement of fact. These three things combined, as well as the fact that negative ions tend to dispel stress and create overall relaxation of the body, definitely promote increased spirituality. Thus we are poised for experiential encounters with God! Since "big business" and "big government" have done such a devastatingly effective job of destroying the ionic balance, it behooves us to do everything we can to restore negative ions to the proper balance; not only to feel better physically but to feel and experience the **energies of God** at the optimal level!

EXERCISE

If you cannot afford a negative ionizer, visit the beach, a river, or a waterfall. Note if you are in a better mood while there, as opposed to before you arrived. Does your energy level feel higher? Do you feel happier and more joyful? Are you more relaxed? Do you feel the presence of God?

CHAPTER 16

Using Piezoelectric Minerals To Sense The Power And Presence Of God

The Piezoelectric minerals are of the quartz family and includes clear, (often white), Amethyst (violet or purple), Aventurine (green), rose, (pink), Aqua Aura (blue), Citrine (yellow or orange), Smoky Quartz (charcoal gray), Rutilated Quartz (clear with gold colored rods), Tourmalinated Quartz (clear with black rods of Tourmaline), Jaspers and Agates. The Topaz family is also included in this piezoelectric group and includes clear or White Topaz, Blue Topaz, Imperial Topaz (orange), and Smoky Topaz (charcoal gray). Tourmaline is also included with these minerals and includes clear or White Tourmaline, Verdelite Tourmaline (green), Rubellite Tourmaline (dark pink//reddish), Indicolite Tourmaline (blue), and Black Tourmaline. Tourmaline is sometimes found with several distinct colors contained within a piece or rod, and usually comprised of Verdelite and Rubellite and sometimes Indicolite; this is called Watermelon Tourmaline.

The thing that makes the PIEZOELECTRIC STONES SO SPECIAL IS THEIR ABILITY TO CONSTANTLY PRODUCE ENERGY which is ELECTRICAL in nature. This is a very difficult concept for many people to accept. This energy is released in a balanced, constant manner except when the Piezoelectric minerals are stimulated by some outside force or presence. This Piezoelectric charge can be measured with an Electrometer, photographed with Kirilian or magnetic field sensing devices, and detected with dowsing rods (previously discussed in regard to Leylines). Another amazing aspect of this piezoelectric energy is that the HUMAN BODY IS ALSO PIEZO-ELECTRIC!!.

There is a kind of natural SYMPATHETIC RESONANCE BETWEEN PIEZOELECTRIC MINERALS AND THE HUMAN BODY. Even though these stones and the body resonate at a different frequency, they both seem to be able to MUTUALLY AFFECT AND ALTER EACH OTHER! There is also a sympathetic resonance between the mineral Quartz and pyramids since they both resonate at 11 GHz!

But how is this possible? That is hard to fully answer other than it is part of the **"great plan" of the Creator, and not just a random/ chaotic occurrence. See Dr. Newton's,** *"A Map to Healing and Your Essential Divinity Through Theta Consciousness,* **for a fuller explanation of this concept in Chapter One.**

What is known by both the author's research, and that of many other crystallographers, it has been repeatedly demonstrated that these minerals become more optically clear after a period of exposure to a person over a period of regular handling or holding. This is most dramatically evidenced when a stone is used repeatedly in prayer or meditation. This remains true even for non-Piezoelectric minerals such as Lapis and Sugulite. This would provide **anecdotal evidence of a sympathetic field of resonance between Quartz and the other minerals with humans!**

It is also known from the experience of many crystal energetic practitioners, that crystals or gemstones can become optically murky or lose some of their color or color intensity when used repeatedly for healing of the body. Not only do crystals and GEMSTONES have the ability to energize and heal our bodies, in many cases they PRODUCE AN OVERALL EMOTIONAL AND MENTAL BALANCING FOR NERVOUS, DEPRESSED, ANGRY, or hyperactive PEOPLE!

Through the simple act of holding a piezoelectric mineral in your hand, there is often a relaxed state which manifests in an individual coupled with altered brain waves and consciousness in the Alpha, Theta, and Delta range. As with the pyramid, these changes can be measured with and EEG machine. We have previously discussed that these are the levels at which deeper meditation and God consciousness occur.

Where this truly remarkable Piezoelectric energy comes from cannot be empirically proven at this time, other than it emanates from the "atomic field". However, **since the Piezoelectric minerals have a relatively constant rate of vibration and resonance, it can be reasonably concluded that the physical body must intuitively and sympathetically attune to these substances through the medium of God, since the Creator's essence is essentially electromagnetic in its nature!**.

The reverse would also be true of the mineral's attunement to man, through an inverse process. Also, since Piezoelectric minerals generate and attract Negative Ions there may be a natural intuitive "movement" by the body which allows it to synchronize with anything that bathes it in Negative Ions. There would be a natural attraction to the emotional and mental balancing achieved when in contact with Negative Ions, as well as a need for the body to assimilate these ions to help rebuild and restore its form or to optimize that form to an essence of "light" or "enlightenment!.

Surely, there will be many people who point out that all of the foregoing discussion is just "folk lore" or wildly imaginative "fairy tales". Furthermore, there will be people who state that the use of these minerals is unnecessary or that they are devious instruments of the devil, which allow us to become possessed with all manner of "negative entities". Yet, even ignoring the scientific and empirically measurable effects that Piezoelectric minerals have on man, it should be recognized that these stones have been used by most of the World's religions and monarchs at one time or another and actually used rather continually!. For the Western religious traditions, many of these minerals were an integral part of the famed "Breastplate" and "The Arch of the Covenant".

Furthermore, some of these minerals are still used by Catholic priests even today, especially Amethyst. While the priests may no longer know the properties or reasons for the effectiveness of these stones, the origins of information can be traced back to the early Hebraic traditions and before that in the Hermetic/Egyptian traditions. These minerals are also part of many Eastern religious traditions including Hindu and ancient Chinese traditions,

SO, WHAT WE HAVE IS A SYNCHRONUS TRADITION OF USING MINERALS IN RELIGIOUS CEREMONIES AND BY THE MONARCHIES OF THE WORLD, THAT FAR EXCEEDS ANYTHING REMOTELY ASSOCIATED WITH RANDOM OR AN ANOMALOUS OCCURENCE!!

How are these minerals used, in a practical application? The answer and process involved is actually very simple. For all Piezoelectric minerals and the non-Piezoelectric stones covered in the next chapter, for most people they are held or loosely grasped in the LEFT HAND. For at least ninety percent of the population, this is the RECEPTIVE HAND THROUGH WHICH WE CAN EXPERIENCE THE ENERGIES OF THE CREATOR!

This was well known in the Hermetic traditions and depicted numerously in the Egyptian hieroglyphs. For some left handed people, because of a reversed body polarity, the receptive hand will be switched to the right hand.

When minerals have points associated with them, such as often occurs in Quartz, Topaz, and Tourmaline, they will specifically direct their energy in the direction of the termination (point). Generally, when holding these points in the hand, they are pointed toward the arm in order to get the full benefit of the electromagnetic energy being released, so that they may be assimilated by the body. These minerals can also benefit us by wearing them as a pendant over the throat or heart Chakras. Furthermore, they can be placed or taped on the appropriate Chakra or gland associated with each mineral and color. This information is compiled in a chart at the end of this chapter.

In addition to the colors involved, the actual chemical composition of gemstone will modify their energy and how they affect the physical body, emotions, and the mind's ability to access the God Energies. Thus, while clear Quartz is pure Silicon Dioxide, Aventurine Quartz is Silicon Dioxide with the addition of Mica, and Rutilated Quartz is Silicon Dioxide with Titanium strands.

Let us now examine the piezoelectric minerals individually:

While the Quartz family has received the most exposure from the media and books, they have the lowest piezoelectric charge of the three families Piezoelectric minerals involved. Yet, they can greatly aid an individual in attuning to God. Clear, or White Quartz, is known to have an overall balancing effect on the body, emotions, and mind.

As has been previously covered, these are known qualities which allow us a fuller access to God. Clear Quartz is comprised of SILICON DIOXIDE which is FOUND also in the HUMAN BODY. Thus, WE HAVE ANOTHER FACTOR WHICH SUPPORTS THE SYMPATHETIC RESONANCE FACTOR, discussed earlier in this chapter.

Amethyst Quartz has been known for thousands of years as a spiritually uplifting mineral. For people with uneven temperaments, this stone will tend to lessen and balance "emotional seesawing". Emotional imbalance is known to impede or prevent any significant interchange with God. For people with a desire to know God more intimately, amethyst tends to focus their thoughts in the direction of God. This not only occurs because of brain wave/consciousness synchronization at the Alpha, Theta, and Delta levels, but also from the violet or purple color of Amethyst. In Eastern religious traditions, violet and purple have been strongly associated with the crown Chakra and the pituitary gland, the energy center and endocrine gland, and is known to improve and facilitate our alignment with God and heal and detoxify the body.

Aventurine Quartz, with its green color and Thymus gland stimulation, and Rose Quartz, with its pink or rose color, are both known to stimulate the Heart Chakra. Both of these minerals relax this area of the body and allow us to more profoundly feel the love within which God is constantly bathing us. In the same manner, these stones are constantly sending "loving" energy to us which we can literally feel in our Hearts. Aventurine and Rose Quartz can also soothe a "broken heart" from a relationship gone astray or terminated

"Aqua Aura" Quartz, also known as "Russian Blue" is Clear Quartz which has been infused with a coating of Gold, which helps to facilitate the blue color change it assumes. "Aqua Aura" quartz is very energizing since its existing piezoelectric properties are augmented with Gold, unleashing a higher level of energy that than Quartz by itself. The blue coloration this Quartz makes it effective in calming the emotions and the mind. It stimulates the throat Chakra and the thyroid gland, as well as secondarily affecting the brow Chakra and the pineal Gland. Because of the balancing aspects of the blue color and the endocrine gland stimulation, "Aqua Aura" greatly facilitates our contacting God in a more effective, meaningful manner.

Citrine Quartz has a tendency to create happiness and joy wearer because of the yellow or orange colors. It activates the Solar Plexus Chakras\ and the Spleen and Adrenal Glands primarily and the Crown Chakra and Pituitary Gland secondarily. While the joy and happiness aspects of Citrine Quartz can obviously help balance the emotions,

Citrine also detoxifies the middle organs in the body and helps to fortify and balance the mind. The result of these multiple effects is that Citrine allows us to more easily align with our "higher self" or "soul", and to energize the body. These things then, allow us to more fully access the power and presence of God.

Smoky quartz, like Citrine, also activates the middle organs. It affects the Solar Plexus Chakra and Adrenal Glands primarily and secondarily affects the root and Spleen Chakra and Gonads and the Spleen. Smoky Quartz can stimulate the increased flow of the Life Force Energies. It can also absorb emotional and mental negativity, and as such, can keep us in a balanced state of consciousness so that we can be more receptive to God.

Rutilated Quartz is versatile in many ways since it stimulates all of the Chakras and endocrine glands. Most Rutilated Quartz has rods of Titanium running through it and Titanium is very compatible with the physical body and will help mend and detoxify it. Rutilated Quartz is also a very powerful detoxifier and balancer of the emotions. It has a much larger electromagnetic quality than just clear quartz due to the Titanium content. And, this highly electrical nature allows rutilated quartz to powerfully activate the "Life Force" energies of God. Therefore, rutilated quartz provides us with a more powerful Quartz similar to "Aqua Aura" and a stronger "conduit" to God.

Tourmalinated Quartz normally is Clear Quartz with black tourmaline rods inside it. It activates the root, Solar Plexus, and crown Chakras, and the Gonads, Adrenal, and Pituitary glands primarily, and the other Endocrine Glands secondarily. As in Black Tourmaline, which will be discussed in depth in this chapter, Tourmalinated Quartz is extremely effective in dispelling and balancing emotional negativity and trauma. Like Rutilated Quartz, Tourmalinated Quartz also powerfully invokes God's Life Force Energies. This attribute is useful in allowing us to more fully access the presence of God.

Agate and Jasper are both varieties of Chalcedony and are similar to each other. The energies and effects generated by these minerals will vary according to the color in which they present themselves as to which Chakra/Endocrine gland will be affected. For specifics on this, refer to the color chart in Chapter 6 on color therapy. Agates and Jaspers are fairly effective in energizing the body and balancing the emotions.

Topaz has many similar characteristic like Quartz but has even a stronger Piezoelaectric charge than Quartz. Clear Topaz is an all purpose mineral like Clear Quartz. Blue Topaz activates the Brow and Throat Chakras and the Pineal and Thyroid Glands. as, and the pineal and thyroid glands. It is very effective as an emotional balancer against negativity and trauma. It is very effective for emotional balance, especially for negativity and trauma. Furthermore, Blue Topaz helps to awaken and improve psychic and spiritual abilities and thus aligns us more closely and completely with God. Gold Topaz activates the Spleen and Solar Plexus Chakras and the Spleen and Adrenal Glands. It helps us to more closely align ourselves with God by detoxifying and regenerating the physical form (body). This is true, because when we are healthy, we are generally much more likely to be happier, and thus more "in tune"/ aligned with God.

Smoky Topaz works similarly to Smoky Quartz but with just a little more intensity. Refer to the discussion on Smoky Quartz for its specific benefits.

As much energy as is generated by Topaz, even more is associated with the Tourmaline family. Tourmalines are comprised of Sodium Aluminum Borosilicate. All Tourmalines, except Black Tourmaline, contain Lithium, and act as a powerful emotional and physiological cleanser of the heart, blood, body, and emotions. Some of these things can be clearly seen in pictures from Kirilian photography.

In the case of Verdelite (green) and Rubellite (dark pink or reddish) Tourmaline, there is a strong affinity to the heart Chakra and the thymus gland, due to the colors they radiate, and the element Lithium, which both contain. The Lithium strengthens the Heart and Blood physically, and the colors invigorate and produce a heart more receptive to the presence of God and calm the mind/consciousness.

Very powerful "openings" of the Heart can occur when Rubellite and Verdelite Tourmaline are placed on this area of the body. These two Tourmalines present themselves combined in the form of Watermelon Tourmaline. So powerful is the Piezoelectric charge of Tourmaline, that it can open the Heart of even the hardest and most negative person. Despite its value in performing the foregoing things, however, it is sometimes unsettling or not beneficial for some people to wear Tourmaline, such as in a pendant, until an individual has achieved an overall balance of their emotions.

Indicolite Tourmaline, however, can work to produce emotional balance, because of its blue coloration. This mineral resonates with the Throat and Brow Chakras, activating the Thyroid and Pineal Glands. Indicolite will best perform the process of emotional balancing by using it in conjunction with the throat and brow Chakras.

Black Tourmaline, although it does not contain Lithium, is nevertheless very powerful in balancing and mending a broken heart. This is because it eliminates negative emotions and depression from a person. These functions are the result of the color black, which is well known to absorb negativity, and is facilitated even more by the powerful Piezoelectric energy charge contained in Black Tourmaline. Black Tourmaline resonates in conjunction with all of the Chakras, glands and organs. But, it works best against negative emotions and depression when used on the Solar Plexus and Heart Chakras.

Lepidolite, although not a Tourmaline itself, is often found with Rubellite Tourmaline rods embedded in it. Both the Lepidolite and Rubellite contain significant amounts of Lithium and will function similarly to Verdelite and Rubellite Tourmaline.

So, you may ask, how can opening your Heart and the elimination negativity and depression from your thoughts, lead to God Consciousness? Again, the answer is quite simple in that UNBALANCED EMOTIONAL STATES OF CONSCIOUSNESS DIRECTLY PREVENT US FROM PERCEIVING AND ACKNOWLEDGING GOD'S OMNIPRESENCE AND LOVE!!. The opposite of these conditions, such as SATISFACTION AND HAPPINESS BRING US CLOSER TO THE PRESENCE OF OUR CREATOR, especially WHEN OUR HEART IS OPEN/RECEPTIVE.

Is not it interesting that virtually every religious tradition, in the West, tells us that WE LITERALLY FIND GOD WHEN WE HAVE AN "OPEN HEART". Such a condition can be fostered even more by the continual output of Negative Ions, which are generated and attracted by the Tourmaline, Topaz, and Quartz families of minerals. Thus we are blessed, in that our creator, God, has provided us with these wonderful mood enhancing/spiritual tools.

Truly, over a period of time, these seemingly insignificant minerals, the Piezoelectric stones, can and will open our consciousness to God. When these minerals are used in conjunction with a meditation session while wearing a Pyramid on our head, the levels to which we can ascend are often greatly increased.

EXERCISE

If this is your first experience with the piezoelectric minerals, visit a crystal or lapidary shop and purchase a piece of Clear Quartz. Place it in your left hand (for some "lefties" you will find that your right hand works better in this exercise) and holding it in a relaxing manner, see if you can detect a warmth, tingling, electricity or pulsation effects in the hand. This is usually a subtle experience, so don't expect to receive a strong electrical shock. If after several minutes you cannot feel anything, then take the Quartz and place it between either your middle finger and thumb, or index finger and thumb. Do not hold the Quartz with a "death grip", since the object of the exercise is to stay relaxed.

Now, place the stone in your hand again and "pump it" by squeezing and relaxing it for about thirty to sixty seconds. Note any sensations that might occur. Once you have experienced "feedback" from your Quartz crystal, undertake a meditation exercise and hold the crystal in the appropriate hand. Try to meditate for at least fifteen to thirty minutes, and note any sensations going on within the body. Do you feel more energized than meditating without a crystal? Do you feel physically lighter? Are you feeling more of God's electromagnetic energies around or within you? Are you more able to commune with God?

For another experience, pick and purchase another Piezoelectric mineral or minerals discussed in this chapter. Make this choice by intuition and not just because it is just the prettiest mineral. Go through the same processes and examination as previously listed.

ON THE FOLLOWING PAGES IS THE GEMSTONE SPIRITUAL PURPOSE CHART

MINERAL/GEMSTONE SPIRITUAL PURPOSE CHART

MINERAL:	CHAKRA:	GLAND/ ORGAN:	#VIBRATION:	SPIRITUAL VALUE:
Amethyst:	Crown/Brow	Pituitary/Pineal	3	Meditation/ intuition/ Divine Love/ inspire
Sugulite:	Crown/Brow	Pituitary/Pineal	3	Same as Amethyst
Purple Fluorite:	Crown	Pituitary		Same as Amethyst but not as strong
Charoite:	Crown	Pituitary	3	Same as Amethyst
White Diamond:	Crown-All	Pituitary-root	5	Very spiritual/ Philosopher's Stone/uplifting
Opal:	Crown/Brow	Pit./Pin.	2	Intuition/God Consciousness
Tanzanite:	Crown/Brow	Pit./Pin.	3	Similar to Opal but more powerful
Tourmalinated Quartz:	Crown-Root	Pituitary— Gonads	3-9	Balances Emotions/Elim. Negativity/ Energizing
Alexandrite:	Crown	Pituitary	5	Spiritual transform/ Regenerative
Lapis Lazuli:	Brow/Throat	Pineal-Thyroid	4-6	Enhances intuition/ Commune with God
"Aqua Aura"/ "Russian Blue Quartz:	Throat	Thyroid	4-6	Spiritual transf./ Very energizing
Sapphire:	Brow/Throat	Pineal-Thyroid	4-6	Attracts/ expandsGod realization

Sodalite:	Brow/Throat	Pineal-Thyroid	4-6	Similar to Lapis but not as strong
Azurite:	Brow/Throat	Pineal-Thyroid	4-6	enhances "Life Force"/ intuition/ Copper infused
Kyanite:	Brow/Throat	Pineal-Thyroid	4-6	Spiritual transf./ calming
Indicolite Tourmaline:	Brow/Throat	Pineal-Thyroid	4-6	Similar to Kyan. but more power
Blue Topaz:	Throat	Thyroid	4-6	Calming/ intuitn.
Aquamarine Beryl:	Throat	Thyroid	4-6	Intuition/calmg.
Turquoise:	Throat/Heart	Thyroid/ Thymus	4.6.7	Meditation/ emotl. Bal./ Energizing
Chrysocolla:	Throat/Heart	Thyroid/ Thymus	4.6.7	Very similar to Turquoise
Adventurine Quartz:	Heart	Thymus	7	Love/healing/ soothes Heart
Rose Quartz:	Heart	Thymus/Heart	3,6,9	Love/soothes
Emerald:	Heart/Solar plexus	Thymus/ Adrenals	7	Emotional bal./ love/healing/ God attunemt.
Tsavorite Garnet:	Heart	Thymus/ Adrenals	7	Similar to Emerald
Malachite:	Heart/Solar plexus	Pineal-Adrenals	7	Activates entire body with "Life Force"
Pink Kunzite:	Brow/Heart	Thymus	6.9	Love, spirit. intuition
Lepidolite:	Heart	Thymus	3	Emotional/ Mental bal./ Joy/happy

Moldavite:	Brow/Heart	Pineal-Thymus	2,7	Spiritually uplifting/ intuitive
Green Jade:	Heart	Thymus	2,7	Unconditional Love/Divinity
Verdelite Tourmaline:	Heart	Thymus	7	Love/healing/ energy
Rubelite Tourmaline:	Heart-Root	Thymus-Gonads	3,6,9	Similar to Verdelite
Watermelon Tourmaline:	Heart-Root	Thymus-Gonads	3,6,9	Energies of Verdel. & Rubel.
Citrine:	Crown-Solar plexus	Pituitary-Adrenals	1	Same as Quartz/ Lepidol.
Yellow Diamond:	Crown-Solar plexus	Pituitary-Adrenals	1	Similar to Citrine/ Spiritual Insight
Peridot:	Heart-Spleen	Adrenals-Spleen	2	Intuition/ Spiritual Awaking
Imperial Topaz:	Solar plexus-Spleen	Adrenals-Spleen	1	Spiritual upliftment & awaken
Amber:	Solar plexus-Spleen	Adrenals-Spleen	1	Spiritual Awaken & balance
Ruby:	Thymus-Root	Gonads	9	Spiritual Courage & devotion
Rhodonite (Red Garnet):	Crown-Thymus	Pituitary-Gonads	9	Spiritual awakening & Love
Bloodstone:	Heart-Root	Thymus-Gonads	9	Similar to Ruby
Black Tourmaline:	Crown-Root	All	8	Eliminate negativity/ soothes emotions

Smokey Quartz:	Crown-Root	All	8	Same as Blk. Tour. but less powerful
Obsidian:	Crown-Root	All	8	like smky. Quartz
Rutilated Quartz:	Crown-Root	All	All	Life force & mental force
Pearl:	Crown-Root	All	All	Emot. bal./ soothing
Zircon:	Crown-Root	All	Depends on color	Similar to Diamond but weaker

This chart should be used as a general guideline. If your intuition and experiences vary from the chart, they should be given greater authority. To figure your numerological vibration number, take all of the digits of your date of birth and add them together to arrive at a single number digit. For example, if you birth date is 21, then your numerological vibration would be 2 plus 1 which = 3.

In the following chapter, we will discuss the non-piezoelectric minerals. The above chart should be referenced for both this and the following chapter.

EXERCISE

Purchase a piece of rose quartz and black tourmaline. When you are experiencing a "broken" or "betrayed" heart, place the rose quartz on your heart, and notice what happens? Does your heart feel more open or balanced, and has the pain left your heart? Now, take a piece of black Tourmaline and place it on your heart. Go through the same process of examination and observation as for rose quartz.

When you are angry, fearful, or upset about something, take a piece of black tourmaline and place it on the solar plexus Chakra (just below the rib cage and above the belly button). Does the anger still reside within you or has it been taken away after several minutes of usage? If it still remains, take another piece of black tourmaline or a piece of rose quartz and place them on your heart simultaneously. You may need to either lie down or tape the minerals to your body. Do you feel better now? Relax as much as you can! Do you begin to feel God's electromagnetic presence, even slightly, in your body?

EXERCISE

Experiment with minerals in different combinations. You can use the chart provided or follow your intuition to decide. Remember that these are aids to attuning to God! They are not an end in and of themselves

CHAPTER 17

Using Non-Piezoelectric Minerals
To Increase Our Divinity

Even though we may not *feel anything* from other minerals that are not Piezo-electrically charged, they nevertheless can magnify God's presence in our lives on all levels; physical, emotional, mental, and spiritual. Although they lack the Piezo-electric properties, they are still infused with the electromagnetic energies of God. In the preceding chapter, we discussed the Lithium content in Tourmaline and Lepidolite. Lithium infused mineral is Kunzite. This mineral is also a powerful purifier of the blood and heart. Kunzite helps an individual to create balance on the physical, emotional, and mental levels. It is very effective in counteracting depression. Since Kunzite resonates with the Heart Chakra and the Thymus gland, it can make the Heart more receptive to the influx of God's energies.

The Beryl family is comprised of several different minerals. Many of the minerals in this family appear to affect the level on which the brain functions, allowing access to the Alpha, Theta, and Delta ranges of God Consciousness. Aquamarine is a Beryl that is an excellent aid to use in conjunction with prayer and meditation. It stimulates the throat and heart Chakras as well as the Thyroid and Thymus glands.

Emerald is another Beryl that functions powerfully in meditation. It also strengthens the back and spine when applied to the area of pain or weakness.

These benefits to the spine cannot be overemphasized, since it is well known in both Taoism and Kundalini Yoga, a misaligned Spine will act to partially block the life force energies of God. While Aquamarine will open the Heart to God, Emerald is even more effective in this function. Emerald's primary function is in activating the Heart Chakra and Thymus gland.

The Diamond is probably the most perfect and powerful mineral that we have on earth today, even though it is not Piezoelectric. Everyone knows that Diamonds are the hardest of the minerals, probably because of its tetrahedral crystalline shape on the atomic level, yet few people know that the Diamond has been known as the "Philosophers Stone" for thousands of years. The Diamond most powerfully activates the crown Chakra, and at the same time, affects all of the other Chakras. It also most powerfully activates the Pituitary gland and additionally, activates all of the remaining glands. When a Diamond is placed on top of the head, it can facilitate extremely intense prayer and meditation sessions, allowing us to more profoundly access God's energies. The Diamond, however, is best used by those individuals who have already begun to open themselves to accepting and experiencing God's presence. For this reason, it is necessary to be able to truly relax in order to receive *feedback* (electromagnetic energies) from the Diamond.

For those people who do not fit within the parameters just discussed, Zircon should be substituted for Diamond, since Zircon is a "cousin" to Diamond. Zircon works in much the same manner as Diamond but with less force. This makes Zircon more compatible for those people who are at the beginning of their quest in experiencing the energies of the Creator. It is a good choice for meditation since it effectuates a greater relaxation than will a Diamond. The importance of relaxation to detecting and experiencing God has been discussed many times previously in this book.

There are two minerals, Lapis Lazuli and Sugilite, which are very significant in their ability to increase our intuition and thus our ability to access the spiritual planes of God. In fact, Lapis has been called the "Seer's Stone" for thousands of years. The followers of many different religions over the ages have used Lapis to enlarge their spiritual boundaries and perceptions of God. Because of its blue color, Lapis strongly resonates with the Throat and Brow Chakras. However, it is used most effectively and powerfully on the Brow Chakra or held in the left hand (for most people). Lapis activates the Thyroid and Pineal glands. Lapis that contains Pyrite, usually present in Afghani Lapis, is even more energizing and effective because of the Orgone effect generated by the presence of this metal. When using Lapis, you can experience a "lightness" in the head and a feeling of being pulled upward. When this phenomenon is experienced, it is an indicator that you are beginning to access God's presence and energies.

Sugilite is a mineral which has been discovered within the last few years. It ranges in color from various hues of purple, lavender, hot pink, and blue. Also known as "Royal Lavulite", Sugilite has essentially the same properties and effects as Lapis, although it works more in conjunction with the brow, crown, and heart Chakras. It stimulates the Pineal, Pituitary, and Thymus glands. It works well on all of the Chakras listed, and is also effectively used in the hand. Besides the "light headed" and "uplifting" phenomenon associated with Lapis, Sugilite also creates a very expansive feeling in the heart of many people, which allows them to more fully access God's love.

Purple Fluorite and Charoite are two minerals that will activate the Crown Chakra and Pituitary gland. Although they are not Piezoelectric, they nevertheless will stimulate the mental centers and activate the spiritual intent within individuals. Opal also activates the crown and brow Chakras and the brow center. Since both the Pituitary and Pineal glands are affected, there is an activation of these spiritual glands which can increase our spiritual intent and desires.

Alexandrite also stimulates the Crown Chakra and Pituitary gland. Being almost as powerful as a Diamond, Alexandrite creates spiritual transformation and growth. It works well either on the head or held in the Hand. Tanzanite has similar properties to Alexandrite as well as affecting the Brow Chakra and Pineal gland. Both Tanzanite and Alexandrite are powerful meditation stones for deep experiences in feeling God at more profound levels. Thus, they are for more advanced practitioners of meditation.

Sapphire is generally a dark blue mineral that affects the Brow and Throat Chakras. It also affects the Pineal and Thyroid glands. Only Diamond is a more perfect gemstone than Sapphire. Unlike Diamond, however, Sapphire will allow its user to more easily access the spiritual planes of consciousness, even without a pre-existing higher level of spiritual understanding. Sapphire is invaluable for calming the mind and emotions for Numerological vibrations corresponding with numbers "four" or "eight". It also balances the Astrological vibrations related to Scorpio, Taurus, Aries and Capricorn. Since these are inherently emotionally unstable Astrological and Numerological aspects, it is beneficial for those people, such as the author, to have these insights. Sapphire attracts and expands "God Consciousness" when used on either the Throat, Forehead or the Hand.

Sodalite works similarly to Lapis but with less energy and results. Kyanite resonates with the Throat and Brow Chakras and the Thyroid and Pineal glands. Kyanite has an overall calming effect for the emotions and is spiritually uplifting.

There is a group of stones, containing the metal Copper, which catalyze and attract the life force energies of God into our bodies. One mineral of this group is Azurite. This was considered a very valuable stone in the Edgar Cayce readings because of the "life force" augmentation it creates and the enhanced intuitive abilities that allow access to the spiritual planes. Azurite activates the Throat and Brow Chakras and the Thyroid and Pineal Glands.

Another Copper influenced mineral is Chrysocolla. It resonates with the Throat and Heart Chakras, as does Turquoise. Both of these similar looking minerals activate the Thyroid and Thymus glands. Chrysochola and Turquoise are good stones for meditation, emotional balance, and increasing the" life force" energies of God.

The last of these Copper effected minerals is Malachite. Malachite affects the heart and Solar Plexus Chakras and the Thymus and Adrenal glands. There also appears to be an activation of the Pineal and Pituitary glands and the Brow and Crown Chakras. Malachite strengthens and activates the entire body with God's life force energies. Being green, it also will powerfully open the Heart to God's love. With all four of the Copper influenced minerals, the increased life force energies that they catalyze and attract, not only creates a fuller access to God's power and presence, but brings about a more blissful or euphoric state of being. This later effect would most likely be related to the release of endorphins—mind altering, mood lifting, pain killing substances secreted by the brain. In such a state of optimum functioning as has been just described our experience of God consciousness increases and is lengthened.

Fluorite also positively affects mental clarity and functioning as well as the more generally known attributes of strengthening Bones and Teeth. The mental clarity is a pathway that can allow us to access the spiritual planes of existence, where God can be most readily and powerfully experienced. Fluorite activates Chakras and Endocrine Glands in relation to the various colors in which it displays itself. (consult color chart for specifics.)

Tsavorite Garnet resonates with the Heart Chakra and the Thymus gland, and expresses many of the same qualities as Emerald. Moldavite also stimulates the Heart Chakra and Thymus gland as well as the Brow Chakra and the Pineal Gland. This stone is very spiritually uplifting and develops spiritual intuition. Thus it can very directly produce states of God consciousness.

Green Jade likewise activates the Heart Chakra and Thymus gland because this mineral can relax and open the heart, and can allow us access to God's divinity.

Moonstone also activates the heart and develops spiritual intuition.

Yellow Diamond is similar in properties as Citrine Quartz in that it resonates with the solar plexus and Crown Chakras and the adrenal and pituitary glands. Yellow Diamond stimulates spiritual insight as well as the joy, happiness, mental balance, and clarity, qualities of Citrine.

Peridot activates the Spleenic, Solar Plexus, and Heart Chakras. It also stimulates the Spleen, Adrenals, and Thymus glands. Not only does it open the Heart to God's love, it also catalyzes spiritual intuition and understanding.

Amber has the same characteristics as Peridot, minus the Heart qualities and attributes.

Ruby is Corundum based mineral similar to Sapphire, which activates the Root and Heart Chakras as well as the Gonads and Adrenal glands. Ruby can open the heart to God's love and creates spiritual courage and devotion.

Rhodolite (red) Garnet has the same properties of Ruby, with the additional characteristics of stimulating the Crown Chakra and pituitary gland. Red Garnet can create spiritual awakening in its user.

Bloodstone works very similarly to Ruby.

Obsidian functions similarly to smoky quartz, in that it absorbs and/or blocks emotional trauma and negativity. It stimulates all of the Chakras and glands as does Pearl. Pearl has qualities of overall soothing and emotional balance.

Now that we have discussed and charted these minerals, the minerals that have the best resonance with each number vibration, as determined by birth date (sum of the day numbers). If your experiences and intuition differ with this generalized chart, then allow your personal feelings to take preference.

ON THE FOLLOLWING PAGE IS THE NUMEROLOGICAL GEMSTONE CHART:

NUMERIOLOGICAL GEMSTONE RESONANCE CHART:

NUMEROLOGICAL PERSONALITY TYPE:	CORRESPONDING GEMSTONES:
Number One:	Imperial Topaz, amber, Citrine Quartz, Yellow Diamond
Number Two:	Pearl, Opal, Moonstone, Peridot, Light Green Jade
Number Three:	Amethyst Quartz, Sugilite, Purple Fluorite, Charoite, Pink Kunzite Rose Quartz, Rubellite Tourmaline, Lepidolite, Tanzanite, Tourmalinated Quartz
Number Four:	Sapphire, Lapis Lazuli, Sodalite, Azurite, Indicolite Tourmaline, Kyanite, Aqua Aura Quartz
Number Five:	White (clear) Diamond, Alexandrite, Rutilated Quartz, Herkimer Diamond Quartz
Number Six:	Turquoise, Chrysochola, Emerald, Tsavorite (Green Tourmalinated Quartz, Pink Kunzite, Rubellite Tourmaline
Number Seven:	Moonstone, Pearl, Green Agate. Aventurine Quartz, Emerald, Tsavorite, Malachite, Moldavite
Number Eight:	Black Tourmaline, Smokey Quartz, Obsidian, Black Pearl, Black Diamond, Amethyst Quartz, Charoitie, Sugilite, Purple Fluorite
Number Nine:	Ruby, Rhodolite (Red Garnet), Bloodstone, Rose Quartz, Pink Kunzite, Rubellite Tourmaline

If we desired to calm and balance ourselves and increase our spiritual intent and thirsting for experiences with God, we would use gemstones on the indigo/blue spectrum such as "Aqua Aura" (blue) Quartz, Lapis Lazuli, Blue Topaz, Aquamarine Beryl, Azurite, Indicolite (blue) Tourmaline, or Sapphire on the Brow and/or Throat Chakra. The vibrational qualities of indigo/blue would be enhanced by the resulting stimulation of the Pineal and/or Thyroid gland.

If we wished to open the Heart more completely to God's love for us, we would use green gemstones such as Aventurine Quartz, Tsavorite Garnet, Emerald, Malachite, or Verdelite Tourmaline. We could also use pink gemstones such as Rose Quartz, Kunzite, Rubellite Tourmaline, Morganite, Rhodochrosite, or Rhodonite. Or, you could use a piece of Watermelon Tourmaline which would combine the green of Verdelite Tourmaline and the pink/rose of the Rubellite Tourmaline. We would place or wear these gemstones either on the Heart or hold them in our hand.

Those gemstones with the colors of green,/pink through the violet range, have the highest spiritual vibrational qualities, and as such, offers a more likely encounter with the presence of God. Also, you can refer to the previous chapter to find out which color, according to your numerological constitution, allows you to be most balanced and relaxed, and thus able to have more significant experiential encounter with God.

The following chart is a synthesis of the preceding information:

EMOTIONAL/MENTAL AFFECTATIONS
OF GEMSTONES AND COLORS

EMOTIONAL/ MENTAL STATE	COLOR	GEMSTONES
Spiritually uplifting/ awaken life force	Purple	Amethy. Qrtz., Sugilite, Pur. Fluor., Charoite, Lav. Kunz., Tanzanite
Calming/Balancing Spiritual Insight & Learning	Gold/Silver	Pyrite, Rutilated Quartz, Gold, Silver, Hematite
Love/Calming/ Balancing/ Relaxation	Blue/Indigo	Indicolite Tourmaline, Blue Sapphire, Lapis, Sodalite, Azurite, Kyanite, Aqua Aura Quartz, Turquoise, Chrysocolla, Blue Topaz, Aquamarine Beryl
	Green/Pink	Emerald, Tsavorite Garnet, Verdelite Tourmaline, Rubellite Tourmaline, Watermelon Tourmaline, Jade, Moldavite, Peridot, Aventurine Quartz, Rose Qrtz, Pink Kunz., Malachite Rubeulite Tourmaline
Joy/Happiness/ Thanksgiving	Yellow	Citrine Quartz, Yel.Diamond Amber, Imp. Topaz, Yel. Bloodstone, Amber, Yellow Beryl
Spiritual Insight and Development	Orange	Imperia Topaz, Orange Agate
Awaken Life Force Energies/ Sexual Energies	Red	Ruby, Rhodo. Garnet. Bloodstone, Rubelite Tourmaline
Eliminate Negative Thoughts/Emotions	Black	Black Tourmaline, Obsidian, Smoky Quartz, Black Diamond

EXERCISE _____

Use the "Numerological Resonance in Relation With Gemstone" chart to find the gemstones compatible with your number vibration. Then, hold these stones in your hand or place them on the appropriate Chakra (refer to "Gemstone Spiritual Purpose Chart" in previous chapter) and notice if you are more energized, feel spiritually uplifted, or have more spiritual intuition or God consciousness. Next, use one or more of these minerals in a meditation session of at least fifteen minutes and note any and all feedback, images, messages, or communication from God.

EXERCISE _____

Visit a crystal and gem shop or lapidary shop and browse through the shop. As you are looking about, note any minerals you are drawn to. You do not need a "logical reason" for this decision. Most often it is just an "impression" or "drawing feeling" to a particular gem or crystal. In most cases you well find that such stones resonate well with you, or you are in need of, on a physical and emotional, or mental and spiritual level. Meditating with these minerals will most likely deepen your meditative state, the amount of God energies you experience, and messages, communications, and images you receive during your meditation session.

EXERCISE _____

Experiment with the "Emotional/Mental Affectations of Gemstones and Colors" chart and notice if the chart helps you to achieve the desired emotional, mental, or spiritual states of consciousness.

CHAPTER 18

Using Metals To Strengthen The Realization Of God's Presence

Yes, as incredible as it may seem, even metals or combinations of metals can and will invoke the life force energies of God. This knowledge goes back at least to the beginnings of Egypt, more than 10,000 years ago. In Egypt, Copper, Brass, Silver or Gold were not only worn on the body as means to increase the presence of God on those who wore jewelry, these metals were also used in the Pharoh's crowns and staffs to achieve the same augmentation of the life force energies.

As was discussed earlier in regard to Chrysocolla, Azurite, Malachite, and Turquoise, the Copper used in them will increase the flow of electromagnetic energies passing through the Chakras and meridians in the human body. Brass, being a combination of Copper and Zinc, works somewhat more forcefully than Copper alone, in magnifying these life force energies. SILVER, being comprised of TETRAHEDRAL PYRAMIDS on the molecular level, even more powerfully energizes the body than either Copper or Brass.

GOLD however, being comprised of OCTADEDRAL PYRAMIDS on the molecular level, is even more energizing than Copper, Brass, or Silver, and is our MOST ACTIVE METAL ATOMICALLY.

TITANIUM is a modern metal that not only strongly attracts God's energies, it is also helps to remove emotional and physical toxins in the body. And, titanium is so COMPATIBLE WITH THE HUMAN BODY, that tissue and bones will actually gravitate to, and around this metal, when implanted inside the body.

The most interesting and powerful results in attracting the life force or God energies, manifest when we COMBINE METALS, creating an ORGONE PHENOMENON. In Brass, more energy is generated by both Copper and Zinc combined, than the sum total of the energy generated from these metals individually. The Egyptians were knowledgeable in the formulation and use of Electrum, a combination of forty percent Gold and sixty percent Silver. As in brass, there is greater electromagnetic force generated from these metals combined, than from the sum total of the energies generated individually. ELECTRUM GENERATES MUCH MORE ENERGY THAN BRASS, SILVER or GOLD. Electrum was also used as a capstone for the obelisks and in pyramids in Egypt, in order to greatly magnify their electromagnetic energy output.

It was earlier mentioned that various metals were used in jewelry, crowns, and staffs. When they are used in the formulation of scale model pyramids, the electromagnetic effect generated by such pyramids is substantially increased. When these metals, especially Silver, Gold, Titanium, and Electrum, are used in conjunction with the various minerals in jewelry, the same results ensue.

These electromagnetic energies that are generated or attracted by the various metals and combinations thereof, are assimilated more fully by the human body when it is in a state of relaxation. As relaxation is the crucial element since a tense and stress filled body is unable to absorb and benefit from this God energy. Use one of the techniques for relaxation, such as full diaphragmatic breathing, meditation, or one of the endorphin producing techniques.

Thus, it should be clear that God, in its diverse creativity, has given us many means by which to attract the life force energies of God.

EXERCISE _____

Procure a piece of Copper, Brass, Silver, and Gold. It is not necessary to have a large piece, even wires of these metals will suffice. Place the copper in your left hand (right if your polarity is reversed) and experience the electromagnetic energies generated and how they affect you. Perform the same routine with each of the remaining metals. After you have experienced the energies from the individual metals, take a piece of Silver and a piece of Gold and hold them together in your hand. In a fashion, you have recreated a rough approximation of Electrum. Can you feel the increased life force energies being generated? Now take the metal or metals that you feel most comfortable with, hold them in your hand and proceed with a fifteen to thirty minute meditation session. Have your metal(s) helped create a better meditation than usual? Are you more relaxed and open to God?

CHAPTER 19

Lasers And Psychotronic Devices

Lasers and psychotronic devices are recent inventions that may not have been created to increase the God energies, yet nevertheless, they have this effect. The lasers we will be referring to are not the type that cut through materials. We are discussing less dramatic types such as the Melles Griot series of lasers. When an object such as a mineral or a pyramid are bombarded with such a laser, the electrons of the object being stimulated move at a faster rate and thus release more energy. In such a state, these objects radiate this increased electromagnetic energy to their user, thus enhancing the presence of God.

When the HUMAN BODY is BOMBARDED by one of these LASERS, the WAVEFORMS generated STIMULATE the ELECTRONS in the body form. Therefore, all the cells, nerves, blood, bones, and tissue of the BODY RESONATE AT A HIGHER LEVEL. The result is that we are charged with God's electromagnetic energies and better able to attune ourselves to God. Additional information on the Melles Griot lasers is contained in the Paradyne Catalogue from Dr. Fred Bell.

In the case of psychotronic or radionic instruments, they are devices which generate waveform energies so subtle that they cannot be measured by any instrument today. It would be helpful to explain more in depth how such waveform energies of radionics work. At this time however, we know very little other than they can improve or degenerate the health of people, animals, and plants, according to how the radionic energies and frequencies are directed. We can detect the after effects of increased vigor following radionic treatment. The "AIM PROGRAM", by Dr. Steven Lewis, has used radionic frequencies for healing and for the cure of Cancer.

There is also a MAGNIFICATION of human extra-sensory perception (ESP) from EXPOSURE to the CORRECT RADIONIC FREQUENCIES. Psychic and intuitive abilities by which we may better know God are enhanced and magnified. Psychotronic/radionic devices can even be used to generate affirmations that magnify our divinity and oneness with God. More information about radionics is available in *"Radionics Interface With the Ether Fields"*, by Dr. David V. Tansley.

There are two basic designs by which these psychotronic/radionic devices are constructed, A computerized version and a non-computerized model. Both versions are effective for improving health, emotional balance, and expanded God consciousness. the computerized version is faster and easier to operate, but costs about four times more than the non-computerized system. Although both the lasers and psychotronic/radionic devices involve several hundred dollars or more, they are useful in increasing our consciousness of God!

EXERCISE

If your resources allow, and you are interested, purchase a radionic device and use it as per the instructions to improve your health and expand your consciousness. Or, you may want to try the system out by visiting a radionic practitioner if one is available in your area. Measure yourself with dowsing rods and muscle testing to ascertain your physical strength and health before treatment. Be aware of any subtle differences that may occur or expanded psychic abilities and better attunement to God. After one, and then after several radionic treatments, measure your aura (with dowsing rods) and your physical strength (with muscle testing). You could also enroll in the AIM program run by Dr. Steven Lewis.

CHAPTER 20

Far Infra-red and Negative Ions Equals the Richway Bio-mat

The author has recently been introduced to a most amazing device which is FDA approved to treat painful conditions in the body. It is called the Richway Bio-mat and as effective as it is in eliminating painful body conditions, it also will relax the body as nothing the author has ever experienced and greatly aids people with insomnia. It has been experimentally shown to heal many conditions in the body. It has been used by three doctors in Japan to very quickly eliminate Cancer from the body.

The Richway Bio-mat contains Amethyst Quartz (and in some cases Black Tourmaline) energized and heated with an electrical source using many different layers of fabric which create an Orgone effect. The Amethyst Quartz releases far (long) infra-red waves which can penetrate six inches into the body. The Amethyst also releases negative ions, which were previously discussed as being mood enhancers for humans. ADDITIONALLY, THIS MAT, BECAUSE OF ITS EFFECT IN RELAXING THE BODY, WILL MAKE IT CONSIDERABLY EASIER TO MEDITATE AND TO ENTER ALTERED STATES OF CONSCIOUSNESS. So for people having trouble meditating, laying or sitting on this mat will make THE MEDITATIVE STATE VASTLY EASIER TO ACCOMPLISH AS WELL AS ESTABLISHING A DEEPER LEVEL OF MEDITATION, WHEREBY WE CAN PROFOUNDLY EXPERIENCE THE ENERGIES OF OUR CREATOR!!!!

CHAPTER 21

Diet And Nutrition

For overall health and as a means of promoting our spirituality, diet and nutrition are important subjects in which we need awareness. While it can be argued, and accurately so, that man is essentially an electromagnetic force field or ethers or spirit, until we realize completely the nature of our essential "essences," it is necessary to sustain the body physically in order to operate as close as possible at an optimal level. This approach allows us to vastly improve our health and improve our connection with God.

The concepts of diet and nutrition have been outlined in great detail by Jethro Kloss in his book, *Back to Eden* and in *Nourishing the Life Force,* by Richard and Mary-Alice Jafolla. As a fundamental dietary principle, it is highly beneficial to eat natural, whole, unrefined foods as much as possible. Much recent research has shown that highly refined and processed foods not only do a poor job of nourishing the body, they also tend to accumulate therein and become fat and toxins.

It has been demonstrated fairly conclusively that unnatural or refined foods also wind up accumulating and becoming impacted in the Colon, one of the places where bodily nutrients are absorbed. This only complicates the nitrifying process of the body since these refined, unnatural products are not easily absorbed or synthesized by the body, even when the Colon and Intestines are functioning properly. The result of this is usually poor health and a low energy level as we live our lives. Thus there is a low capacity for attuning to the presence of God. This is because the body/"temple" is in no condition to receive, glorify, or "make a joyful noise unto the lord". That is the bad news! The good news is that our "temple", the body, can be restored to its beautiful, optimal condition following natural, whole food diets such as Vegetarian and Ayurvedic practices.

Natural foods include primarily fresh vegetables and fruits, and where this is not possible, than the frozen equivalents. These also include whole grains and legumes such as peas, beans and nuts. Unnatural foods include refined white flour, or refined sugar products such as those derived from cane and sugar beets, corn syrup and high fructose corn syrup and any foodstuffs adulterated with preservatives, dyes, hydrogenated oils and fillers.

Although in the Ayurvedic diet it is permissible to consume dairy products in limited amounts, there is a lot of evidence which shows that pasteurized dairy products are not only hard to digest, but they also make it difficult to digest non-dairy foods eaten at the same time. On the other hand, raw milk and raw milk products are eminently absorbed by the body, because the Lactase enzyme has not been been inactivated/ killed by the Pasteurization process.

It is also known that alcohol, refined sugars (this does not include real maple syrup, molasses, Honey, Stevia, Xylitol and Erithrol), and many drugs flush vitamins and minerals from the body, in a diuretic process, so their ingestion should be minimized or eliminated.

Some people may have been noticed that the issue of meats has been avoided thus far. And that is because this is somewhat of a complicated issue. There is a belief, which probably originated in eastern thought and religion, when we eliminate meats from our diet, the physical body and thought vibrations become more closely attuned to God. While this seems be true, as the Jafolla's discuss in *Nourishing the Life Force,* another factor in this discussion is the that as our spiritual vibration and intent rises, the conscious desire for meat consumption begins to disappear.

Regardless of this, it is known that today's RED MEATS, especially beef, are not only loaded with fat (which Americans already in general have too much of), but are also CONTAIN SIGNIFICANT AMOUNTS OF ANTI-BIOTICS AND STEROIDS. There is much discussion today regarding how detrimental is a diet, loaded with fat. Fat burdens the physical body, and it is possible that this also indirectly becomes a burden on the brain. As the brain-computer and resulting mind-consciousness function inefficiently, spiritual experiences can be denied to those seeking a fuller experience with God.

It is also known that the regular consumption of anti-biotic drugs actually break down the body's immune system defenses. We are just now getting significant feedback of how deadly steroids are to the human body over a period of time. The same thing that can be said about fat would also apply to antibiotics and steroids in regard to brain/mind functions. If one must consume beef, organically produced beef would be the best choice. As to pork, it is one of the most toxic foods which can be eaten and thus should be definitely avoided. Venison is very lean and is not infested with steroids or drugs, and is the preferable red meat for consumption.

Although chicken and turkey are more nourishing in protein, lower in fat, and seemingly less toxic to the body than the red meats. However, much of the poultry today is laced with antibiotics or infested with salmonella bacteria. The feed used for chicken and turkey production is also laced with Arsenic, which is indicated in the pink color of the finished products. And while fish is the lowest in fat of all meats and high in protein, mercury, which is extremely toxic to the body, is found in high concentrations in Tuna. Also, many other contaminants (heavy metals, pollutants, and insecticides) are being detected in other fish.

At the least, it would appear wise to begin to eliminate meat from the diet, beginning with red meats. This is even more important in light of the fact that we now know how contaminated meats are with chemicals, drugs, and insecticides. There is also a disproportionate concentrating and compounding of these toxic foreign substances well beyond the original dosage which has been ingested by such animals as reported several times in the magazine "Vegetarian Times". This can often exceed ten times the original concentration. Whereas with vegetables sprayed with toxic chemicals and insecticides, concentration and compounding usually will usually not more than double. Beyond this, it takes twenty pounds of grain feeds to produce one pound of beef. So unless Cattle are only produced by grazing on grasses, this is an inefficient and wasteful use of precious food stocks!

This naturally leads us to organic food production methods. We have created a condition today where we have over-contaminated our vegetables and fruits with toxic petrochemical insecticides and fertilizers. In a recent book, *Secrets of the Soil,* by Peter Tompkins and Christopher Bird, it has been demonstrated conclusively that fruits and vegetables grown organically—with only natural ingredients—will not only taste better, but are considerably more nutritious. With an organic treatment, the energies of God (life force) become more firmly established in the soil, since natural, instead of synthetic growth stimulants, are used. Thus as GOD'S PRESENCE IS MORE COMPLETELY ESTABLISHED IN THE SOIL, it BECOMES MORE FULLY TRANSFERRED TO FRUITS AND VEGETABLES and THEY BECOME "VITALIZED". When these "vitalized/energized" foods are consumed by the body, it is healthier and fortified additionally with the presence of God, and CAUSES THE BODY TO RESONATE AT A FREQUENCY MORE ALIGNED/ATTUNED YO GOD!

It should also be recognized that many people have food allergies. In fact, almost everyone is allergic to at least several foods, if not more. Whether you do or do not have a food allergy or allergies can be determined by medical tests. However, if you learn to attune to your body, you can detect patterns of poor food digestion or stomach upsets which can indicate problem foods for you. This can be done by a process of elimination. For most people, food allergies cause the accumulation of unnecessary fat on the body as well as poor nutrient assimilation.

Let us consider an example of this where digestion problems are always present after eating shredded wheat with bananas and milk. If you eliminate bananas from the meal and there is still indigestion or an upset stomach, you would then eliminate either the milk or the shredded wheat. Should you find your digestion had improved, you would have discovered the food that you are allergic to. However, if your digestion problem remains after eliminating all three of the foods, then you would most likely know that you were allergic to all of them. And this is often the case. In fact many people are allergic to all three of the foods in our example: bananas, milk, and wheat.

Many people are also allergic to corn and eggs. If there is a food allergy, the way to eliminate it is to stop eating the problem food or foods, for at least several weeks to several months. By doing this, the allergy should go away. And, after it disappears, you may begin to sparingly eat the allergic food, gradually in-creasing your intake.

Many people are Lactose intolerant. And yet when you give these same people dairy products from raw milk, they become digestible in this unpasteurized form. Cooking of food causes all sorts of digestive problems because the food's naturally occurring digestive enzymes, have been destroyed by heat. This is well explained in, *Enzyme Nutrition,* by Dr. Edward Howell. This would then lead to one of two conclusions. Either we should eat our foods, raw—uncooked—or we need digestive enzyme supplementation which includes Protease, Amylase, Lipase and Cellulase for foods that are cooked. The raw food diet would include eating meats uncooked. But this presents other problems such as the proliferations of worms, parasites and bacteria are remaining because they have not been destroyed by the cooking process!

What then, would be a good all around diet? Preferably a healthy diet would include a cross section of fruits, vegetables, whole grains, and cereals. Especially, with breads and cereals, they should be high in fiber. The one to two gram fiber content, per serving, is grossly inadequate. Breads should be at least three or four or eight grams of fiber and cereals should be at least five to ten grams or more of fiber. Not only would this provide you with the proper vitamin and mineral content, it would *also* include lots of fiber which keeps the colon clean and prevents glycemic spikes from sugar compounds. For protein, eat legumes, (including beans, peas, nuts or peanuts) along with fish or poultry.

Care should be taken to eat these foods in order of digestibility: first fruits, next vegetables, then whole grains and cereals, and finally meats. Focusing on alkalizing foods, to keep the body at an alkalized "Ph", 7.1 or higher, will give the body more energy and makes it very difficult for viruses and bacteria's to exist in your body. What has more energy, an alkaline battery or a Nickel-Cadmium battery. The answer which almost everyone knows is the alkaline battery. And since WE ARE A "BATTERY" of sorts, since our bodies are infused by electromagnetic/Pranic energies, a body with an ALKALIZED CONDITION may well transfer the PRANIC ELECTRICITY in an AUGMENTED FORM THROUGHOUT THE BODY! This condition is beneficial for us as we are MORE FULLY MELDED WITH OUR CREATOR, WITH SUBSTANCIALLY IMPROVED "LINES OF COMMUNICATION" therewith!

There are charts available listing the acid–alkaline properties of foods. BE AWARE, THAT WHETHER A FOOD IS RAW OR COOKED, CAN SIGNIFICANTLY ALTER THE "Ph" thereof! One example is Tomatoes. When they are eaten raw, they are alkalizing to our bodies. When they are eaten cooked, they are acidifying!

For beverages, water is your best choice, preferably at least *eight* glasses of water per day. Water is very important, not only in helping to cleanse toxins from the body, it is also important to keep the electromagnetic/Pranic current coursing properly through the body. Drinking water that has been alkalized is beneficial. Drinking water that has been distilled and infused with more oxygen is probably even more beneficial. You can get an H_2O_2 water from "The John Ellis Water Machine" So what you are drinking is more akin to H_2O_2 than H_2O. The implications of this are extremely significant because Oxygen seems to be a tranporter of electricity/Pranic force throughout the body and this just makes us more attuned to our Creator. This is discussed in more depth in Dr. Newton's, *A Map to Healing and Your Essential Divinity.*

After water, natural juices are very beneficial, especially diuretic juices such as Grape, Apple and Cranberry, especially in an organic, unpasteurized form. If milk is to be consumed, it should be done so sparingly or in the raw form, unsparingly. Teas with caffeine, caffeinated coffee, and all carbonated drinks are extremely detrimental to the body in that they flush vitamins and minerals from the body, much like alcohol, sugar, and drugs. Eliminating these items from the diet will provide a more healthy body form.

There is a contrary opinion that a small to moderate use of alcohol on a daily basis is beneficial to the body, and some research supports this position. This outlined in *Healthy Pleasures* by Sorbel and Ornstein. You the reader must make your own decision on this but if alcohol is to be used, let it be done in true moderation. The main benefit of wine is that it contains Resveratrol, which among other things, make it anti-tumoric. You can get this compound through drinking Grape juice and eating Grapes, so we really do not need wine for this! Also there are Resveratrol supplements that are being marketed.

Finally, with beverages, it is best for digestion to limit your intake of liquids to fifteen minutes before and fifteen minutes after meals. For optimum digestion, you should abstain from any beverages during a meal. The question remains however, will such a dietary regimen as suggested provide a closer link with God? The answer is yes, over a period of time, as your health begins to improve and the life force/ Pranic energies more fully course throughout the body. The benefits of this are well explained in Dr. Newton's, *A Map to Healing and Your Essential Divinity. Through Theta Consciousness*

In taking the above suggestions into consideration, always consult a dietitian or doctor before changing your diet. On the other hand, doctors are rarely really informed or have expertise on dietary knowledge Remember, as the body is healthy, so is the mind and the spirit. And as the mind and spirit are healthy, the body normally follows suit. It is the old symbiotic relationship: *As above, so below, and as below, so above.* In the next chapter we will explore vitamin, mineral, and herbal supplements.

ALSO, FOR MORE DISCUSSION OF THESE MATTERS, AS WELL AS LIVING WITHOUT EATING, CHECK THE CHAPTER, "WHAT HAPPENS WHEN THE SHIITE (EXCREMENT)—NOT THE MOSLEM SECT—HITS THE FAN?" IN DR. NEWTON'S BOOK, *A MAP TO HEALING AND YOUR ESSENTIAL DIVINITY.*

EXERCISE

Begin to improve and refine your diet according to this chapter. This should be gradual, ongoing, and with the advice of a dietitian or doctor. Do you feel better, lighter, and more alert mentally and spiritually after being on your new diet? Keep a daily journal of any foods which consistently cause indigestion. When you have determined these according to the process of elimination, consider eliminating them from your diet. Does your digestion improve after doing this? Do you feel better overall?

Also, consider eliminating refined sugar, alcohol, drugs, and caffeine from your diet. As you do this, do you feel more energetic more of the time? Such a program should be done gradually to reduce the possibility of shock or withdrawal to the body. Alkalize and oxygenate your body with foods and water. With such a protocol, you can only get healthier and begin to assume your Divine potential!

CHAPTER 22

Vitamins & Minerals

In the preceding chapter we talked about the importance of a proper diet. Now we will explore the related area of vitamins, minerals, and herbs, which promote health and thereby increase the life force energies. It could reasonably be asked, if we consume a varied and balanced diet, why would such things be necessary? This is a legitimate question, and it centers on the body's ability to assimilate nutrients, and whether in fact it is absorbing the requisite vitamins and minerals from the food it ingests.

Under a situation where there is optimum digestion along with a clean and properly functioning colon, vitamin, mineral, and herbal supplements would not be needed. However, at the present time, and until the body can properly and completely rid itself of the various toxins it produces, it is usually beneficial for most people to take additional supplements.

The reason that these supplements are so important is vitamins A, C, E, along with the minerals zinc and selenium, have been directly related to building a strong immune system in the body. With a stronger immune system, you have greater protection against colds, flu, cancer, and other illnesses. Furthermore, there is strong evidence that herbal folk remedies such as comfrey, Achillea (Yarrow), Echinacea, Goldenseal, and Ginseng, very strongly enhance the immune system.

With so many types of vitamin and mineral supplements, it is difficult for most people to know which one or ones to take. The best rule of thumb in this is that naturally formulated, as opposed to synthetic supplements, will have a substantially higher absorption rate and faster availability for use by the body. Sufficient research has been done at this time show that synthetically formulated vitamins and minerals which accounts for the majority of those produced, are inferior in value for the body.

However, even among naturally produced supplements, there are dramatic differences in potency and availability. Those supplements which are "organically grown" are superior in nutritive value. These would include Dr. Bell's "Excalibur" vitamin and mineral supplement, and "Alpha Full Spectrum" from Mega Food. Check Dr. Newton's "A Map to Healing and Your Essential Divnity Through Theta Consciousness" regarding nutrifying the body with Prana, in Chapter Twelve.

Also of high nutritive value to the body is flower pollen, Bee pollen, and algae based products. Bee and flower pollen are similar, in that bee pollen is just flower pollen that has some Honey and other beneficial substances included by the collecting bees. The pollens are high in protein (35%), and contain vitamins and minerals necessary for the body. They act to remove toxins from the body and help to build the immune system, while at the same time aiding in digestion.

The Algae based products are Chlorella and Spirulina. These are higher in protein than pollens and have about the same vitamin and mineral ingredients. They are also builders of the immune system and help to remove toxins. While all Algae products produced are very good, one in particular appears to be superior in value because of other added ingredients. "Exsula Irridesca", by Life Enthusiast Co-op, is an algal product which contains Spirulina and Chlorella. It includes Chlorophyll and Carotenes, along with royal jelly, Evening Primrose, an antioxidant (which takes care of the free radicals discussed in a previous chapter) which helps to oxygenate the body), co-enzyme 10, massive amounts of fiber, minerals, vitamins, and amino acids and many other herbs. In testing the muscle structure of individuals using "Exsula Irridesca", they are substantially stronger than with any other supplement of any type produced today. Yet as much as the "Exsula" energizes the body with the life force energies of God, it does so in a relaxed, balanced manner.

Another similar product which exceeds its competitors is "Billy's Infinity Greens". This product has everything you will need to be nitrified and detoxified, including probiotics. This company also makes a "power bar" type product that contains Algae's, among many other beneficial nutrients and fiber, and has the most incredibly delicious product in this category.

Some supplements are as important, if not more so, to your emotional health as they are to your physical health. In *Emotions and Your Health,* a book by Emrika Padus and Prevention Magazine, are many detailed studies which show how powerful the B complex vitamins (especially B6 and B12) are in creating a good emotional and mental outlook. Not only does the B complex aid in memory functions, but with a consistent application in double blind studies, there was found substantial relief from those troubled with paranoia and schizophrenia. This was true even in cases which were thought to be incurable by drugs or electroshock therapy. It could even be argued that the B complex is a powerful supplement which can put us in a state of emotional and mental functioning that allows us to more fully tap into God's presence and Pranic energy. There may also be a relationship between this complex supplement and endorphin production. However, this cannot be proven at this time.

Recent research By Dr. Jeffrey A. Fisher, revealed in *The Chromium Program,* has shown us the importance of the trace mineral chromium in our diet. Chromium will not only help eliminate excess body fat, but also helps to produce muscle tissue. Brewer's yeast, Thyme, Black Pepper and Prunes have extremely high concentrations of chromium.

Before chromium can have a significant effect on the body, you must first adopt a diet similar to that listed in this book in Chapter 20.

There are indications from holistic health sciences that as we are fortified physically, emotionally, and mentally, we become more fortified spiritually, and thereby filled with God's life force energies. As such, you should be able to more profoundly access and experience God in your life. Should you decide to include vitamins and minerals in your diet, you will more than likely benefit from them. It is highly recommended that you consult a dietitian or doctor first before adding these items to your daily regimen.

EXERCISE

In conjunction with medical or nutritional advice, institute a program of vitamin and mineral supplements. To get their full benefit, this should be an ongoing practice. Do you feel better after several days? After one month? First, do a test for body/mind improvement for one month with synthetic vitamins and minerals and keep a daily journal of how you feel and perform. Then, do the same thing with natural, organically grown vitamins and minerals. Keep a daily journal for this also. Did you see any improvement or more improvement with the natural organic supplements?

CHAPTER 23

The Role Of Herbal Remedies

Another part of proper diet and nutrition is the use of herbs, flowers, and plants, to increase the life force energies. For thousands of years the Chinese and other oriental peoples have revered the roots of the herb Ginseng. There are four major kinds of ginseng which are listed in order of potency in *Folk Medicine: The Art and Science.* The most potent is Chinese ginseng, followed by Korean, Siberian, and American. There are people however, who feel American Ginseng is the most potent.

Ginseng is not only a powerful physiological energizer of the body, (sometimes used by athletes to enhance their performances in sports) it is also believed by the Chinese to increase longevity, impart wisdom, and improve mental functioning. It should be evident that this herb completely energizes the body on all levels, along with enhancing and activating the inherent divinity in each of us. The natural result of this is that ginseng may well be able help us create a state of being where God naturally becomes a more important and central part of our lives.

This will not happen immediately, but rather as a process of gradual evolution. Much the same could be said for the herb Salvia (Sage), which again is revered by the Chinese for its ability to impart wisdom and spirituality. When Salvia is burned, it is a powerful way to cleanse away lingering and destructive emotions from a person's consciousness. This process of using Sage for cleansing is utilized also in the Native American traditions. Sage activates our mental and spiritual energy centers, and will help to strip away destructive emotions, which cause stress and prevent the energies of God from interacting with the body. It should be certainly considered for use by any spiritual aspirant whose goal is to know God more profoundly, and for those people seeking more emotional tranquility and to dispel negativity, as through "smudging", where the smoke from burning Salvia is used to "cleanse" an area.

The last group of herbs discussed is the Allium family. This includes Chives, Shallots, Onions, and the most powerful of this family, Garlic. All of these herbs work in such a manner as to purify the blood in the body and to eliminate fat/cholesterol. While all of the Alliums are helpful to the body, Garlic is the most beneficial since it also has extremely potent antiseptic and anti-biotic properties. This anti-biotic characteristic is most likely due to the fact that Garlic and all of the other Alliums contain large amounts of Sulfur, which kills viruses and bacteria.

Thus, garlic is extremely effective in fighting infections and in building the body's immune system. Garlic and the other alliums, then, facilitate focusing more of the God force energies by providing for a considerably healthier body. The easiest and most practical way for many people to take garlic is with garlic capsules which are available at most health food stores. Garlic may be up to fifty times stronger than Penecillin and this may be due to the fact that it has a very high concentration of Sulfur. Earlier in this book, we covered the importance of water in the proper functioning of the body. There are also treated water formulas created by Dr. John Wesley Willard, Sr. of CAW Industries. Dr. Willard's catalyst altered water, called "Dr. Willard's Water", is a powerful anti-oxidant, which eliminates free radicals from the human body. These special waters act to remove toxins and to alkalize/energize the physical body, which naturally becomes more divine as it becomes purer. Other waters of this magnitude have been created by Dr. Patrick

Flanagan at Flanagan Research. Flanagan's water is known as "Crystal Energy Concentrate".

There are also natural health and healing remedies including homeopathic remedies, "Bach Flower Essences", and "Perelandra Vegetable and Flower Remedies". Homeopathic remedies are created by transferring a low dosage of a sickness or malady radionically from the source into a vibrational medicine. As opposed to conventional, allopathic medicine, which tries to conquer sickness and disease through giving the body often times toxic, foreign substances to effectuate healing, homeopathy provides the body with a very low dosage of the sickness or disease it is dealing with in order that the body's natural immunity system can fend off the illness. This healing process occurs gradually, but more completely than with conventional medicine. But since it deals with causation rather than effects, it is a lasting healing protocol.

In the case of "Bach Flower Remedies" and "Perelandra Vegetable and Flower Essences", the essence of flowers, plants, or vegetables, are transmitted into "the medicine" in a vibration mode. These natural substances, which are vitally infused with the life force energies of God, (Nature being one of God's purest expressions) work in harmony with, and consideration of, the natural body rhythms and energies. The life force energies of the body are gradually raised to a point where sickness and disease are eliminated. The "Bach" and "Perelandra" remedies are also invaluable for releasing stress and *emotional* negativity stored in the body, which are at the lowest common denominator, responsible for creating sickness *and* disease. This is discussed in detail in Louise L. Hay's book, *You Can Heal Your Life* and in Dr. Robert J. Newton's book, *A Map to Healing and Your Essential Divinity*.

All three of these means of healing effectuate health through respect of the natural body rhythms and cycles and in harmony with the realms of nature created by God. These means and methods are more fully vitalized with the God force energies and are a conduit through which God can be experienced more fully.

EXERCISE _____

Investigate alternative ways of healing and health maintenance such as discussed in this chapter. It would be well advised to consult with an herbalist, a naturopathic doctor, or homeopathic practitioner prior to adding these herbal remedies to your regimen. Consider using some of the herbs and products listed in this and the previous chapter to fortify your immune system and increase your life force energies. Keep a daily journal for at least one month and make notes of which herbs/substances seem to benefit you the most.

CHAPTER 24

Making The Body Supple And Receptive To God

Deep tissue massage, such as Rolfing and Postural Integration, are also methods by which we can enhance the life force energies of God. Even the more surface type massage techniques such as Swedish massage have life force benefits. By loosening the muscles (basically bands of energy), stress and tension are reduced in the body, thus allowing the electromagnetic energies and presence of God to be more fully experienced. The complete benefits of deep tissue techniques include a softening of the muscles and consequently a release of stress and tension.

As muscles are loosened and tension is relieved from them, bones and vertebrae will once again assume a more optimal alignment. This is another benefit of deep tissue massage. In the case of spinal alignment, the more perfectly the vertebrae in the spinal column are arranged, more of God's life force energies can enter into the body and thereby provide us with a greater opportunity to know God on a significantly more meaningful level. Spinal alignment is a primary preoccupation of Chiropractic discipline. As such, Chiropractic techniques are very beneficial in our pursuit of knowing God more intimately.

Still another benefit of deep tissue massage, aside from the elimination of bodily pain, is an opportunity to release negative emotions and emotional situations. These emotions are generally the original cause of muscle stiffness and bone or spinal misalignment. As these negative emotions are released, disruptive conditions are removed from the mind. Such negative emotions can even include a perceived estrangement from the caring presence of God. When these emotions are removed, it creates more "room" for God to fill our improved thought process. In other words, we have the opportunity to delete negative, disruptive programming from our internal personal computer—the Brain—and begin to truly experience the reality of God in our lives!

Regardless of the complicated discussions such as are contained in *The Keys of Enoch* and *The Body Electric,* the electromagnetic or etheric energies are augmented and balanced after a treatment in the related disciplines of Reiki, Trager, and polarity balancing. The results experienced are similar, if not the same, as after deep tissue massage, Shiatsu, and Chiropractic alignment. This is often felt as either a "lightness", warmth, tingling, etc., in the body.

If we use these or other related methods, devices, and means to reach out to God, the Creator that is omnipresent, omnipotent, and omniscient, as described by Mary Baker Eddy in *Science and Health with Key to the Scriptures, you* cannot help but enhance and deepen an experiential relationship with God! This is also discussed in more detail in Dr. Newton's other book, *"A Map to Healing and Your Essential Divinity Through Theta Consciousness.*

EXERCISE

Determine through your inner "knowingness" (intuition), which discipline listed here will help you to know God better and then have it performed on your body or perform it yourself. In the case of magnotherapy (discussed in Chapter Thirteen), you will need some polarized magnets or "Nikken" bi-polar magnets and either Dr. Prince's or Dr. Holzapfel's book. After undergoing the process of deep tissue massage, Chiropractic, Shiatsu, polarity balancing, or magnotherapy, note any and all sensations which have transpired. Do you feel lighter, warmer, tingling, etc., in your body or parts thereof? Do you feel more receptive to or cognizant of God? If you are not getting an answer, ask God for guidance.

CHAPTER 25

Bringing It All Together

W e have discussed and covered a considerable number of methods, devices, and means, to raise the life force energies which comprise the aspects and qualities of God. Even though these have been discussed in separate sections, all of these life force/Pranic stimulators work in harmony with each other and the more that they are combined, the more of God's presence can be focused or accumulated, thus making our encounters with God even more significant and powerful.

It is important to create a healthy body through diet, nutrition, supplements (vitamins, minerals, and herbs), and massage or related practices to create a vibrant, energetic, and healthy body, which radiates the life force and thus is more receptive to the presence of God. In conjunction with this, begin to work daily with affirmations and/or subliminal tapes to overcome destructive habits and to increase your spirituality and connection with God. Also start with daily meditation and prayer as has been discussed. Use relaxation techniques such as Tai Chi or Do-In just before a sitting meditation or use Tai Chi as a powerful standing meditation. You might combine Tai Chi or Do-In with a mantra or toning.

Begin your stationary meditations for a short period of time—about 10-15 minutes if you are new to the meditation experience. Gradually increase the length of your meditation to between 30–60 minutes or more if you desire. Remember, meditation can occur even during strenuous activity, especially if you are relaxed and are enjoying yourself.

At the beginning or during your meditation session, you may want to try some mantras, toning, or use Tibetan instruments such as bowls or bells. Or you may want to use a spiritually inspiring musical tape during meditation such as "On Hearing Solar Winds" or "Tibetan Plateau". Your meditation could be enhanced through the use of spiritual incenses such as Sandalwood, Lotus, or Frankincense and Myrrh.

During your meditation you may also want to use one of the Piezoelectric or other gemstones in you left hand or place them on the corresponding chakra centers. You may choose to use several crystals and gemstones together. This is acceptable, since they are all compatible with each other. Combined with some or all of these suggestions, you may want to wear a small pyramid on you head or sit under a larger pyramid during your meditation.

The use of a negative ion generator could do even more to create a euphoric atmosphere to facilitate your meditation to invoke the presence of God. You may also choose to have colors of violet, blue, pink, and green in your meditation space. As you can see, we have a modular system that allows us to combine these methods, devices and means which exponentially allows us to increase the magnitude of God's presence. DO NOT LET ARBITRARY RULES AND PERCEPTIONS TO LIMIT YOUR CREATIVITY and desires as you are searching for ways to more profoundly invoke God's energy in your daily life!

EXERCISE

Let your creativity and imagination "run wild" and combine as many of the things as just discussed into your meditation sessions and into your daily life. Try it, you'll like it! Do not hesitate to experiment and try new combinations which could give you an even greater access to God's power and love.

CHAPTER 26

Does God Give Us Only One Lifetime?

As great controversy will ensue with the release of this book, regarding the many ways in which we perceive and experience God, the author will be even more contentious as we explore questions and concepts about God and its creation, man. One very real question which has received considerable media coverage is, "Does we have only one lifetime?"

This concept of man only possessing one lifetime, is central to the belief system of Christians and Moslems, even though it is known that Mohammed was very interested in reincarnation and Jesus said, "Before Abraham was, I am". These two religions have chosen to isolate themselves from a preponderance of evidence which we have today that would indicate otherwise, that indeed man has multiple lifetimes. One empirical indicator that man reincarnates is through the detailed research done into "near death" experiences.

Elizabeth Kubler-Ross has done detailed studies on near death experiences for many years. There is a haunting recurrence of the same or similar recall, of people who appeared clinically dead, spending some time on the spiritual planes of existence, and returning to relate experiences of being bathed in an intense light. This intense light is just another way that God expresses Itself! Although we are getting somewhat sidetracked from our reincarnation question, these "near death" experiences have also brought us back considerable information related by the "near death" patients, that life is an endless stream of lifetime after lifetime.

Beyond these experiences, we have a preponderance of the acceptance of reincarnation not only in a majority of the world's religions and philosophies, but also in the literature of the ages. This would include such acknowledged great writers such as Shakespeare, Thoreau, and Emerson to name a few. This is exhaustively detailed in, *Reincarnation: The Phoenix Fire Mystery,* by Head and Cranston.

In the Christian tradition, it is a well known fact that the Catholic Church performed a major editing and suppression of certain information contained in Biblical texts. This occurred at "The Council of Nicaea" and was done under coercive death threats to the Pope from a Turkish King, Constantine. And, most of this editing/suppression was in regard to reincarnation. Reincarnation was viewed as something which would lead to lethargy and the lack of striving for excellence in one's individual life. Thus reincarnation was "cast out" of the Bible, even though there are overt references to reincarnation in the Vatican library. One of the covert references to reincarnation that remains extant in the New Testament is when Jesus proclaimed: "Before Abraham was, I AM."

A rather ironic aspect in regard to the Christian and Moslem denial of reincarnation, is that they both expect a return of a "Messiah" like figure. In the case of Christianity this is well known to be Jesus the Christ. However, every other major religion has this aspect of the return of the Messiah including the Aztecs with Quetzalcoatl, Hindus, and Buddhists, among others. If a return of a Messiah is not reincarnation, what is? These concepts are also covered in depth in, *The Wisdom of the Ages,* by Manly P. Hall and also in his book *Reincarnation.* And if it is said that this is only relevant to "ascended Masters", Jesus himself proclaimed: "Greater works than these shall ye do also." While orthodox Christianity conveniently ignores Jesus' behest, neither Mary

Baker Eddy nor the author will be complicit in this lack of self evident perception!

From the fields of the "new sciences", especially quantum physics, we also know that when a person "dies", they leave an energy imprint of themselves which can be measured and detected. WHY WOULD SUCH AN IMPRINT BE LEFT IF IT WERE NOT TO BE USED AT A LATER DATE?

Another case we can make for reincarnation comes from those experiences that reoccur from time to time where we meet someone who we have never known in this lifetime, and yet we are sure we already know/knew them. Or there is a person or persons who we immediately like upon our first meeting, or conversely we hate or intensely dislike for no logical or valid reason. Would not these strong feelings tend to reinforce the **idea** that we have lived before and will live again?

Finally, we have those activities of which we are phobic (afraid of) for no particularly logical reason. Why should we be afraid of heights or of the oceans in this lifetime, if there is absolutely no basis upon which to justify our phobia? Would not this indicate that these phobias are from past lifetime experiences? Many hypnotherapists and psychotherapists have concluded that there must be a basis for reincarnation based on what their patients relate to them while undergoing hypnotic regression therapy. The cases of this occurring are almost endless!

While it may be argued by Christians that reincarnation is a tool of the devil, it is inconceivable to me that all of the great religions, including early Christianity and Islam, are possessed by the devil. If anything, the earlier teachings of Christianity, and for that matter any other religion, are purer and more divinely inspired than the teachings as they are later explained, diluted, edited, suppressed, and reinterpreted incorrectly!

It is also too far-fetched for the author to entertain the idea that the great writers of earth's history, were also possessed by the devil. This concept is even more incredulous when you consider the spiritual devotion to God exhibited in the writings and lives of Emerson, Thoreau, Whittier, and Whitman (Walt, not Meg), to name a few who believed in reincarnation. Thus, from a preponderance of evidence both empirical and circumstantial, it is clear that God provides us with multiple lifetimes, if we wish to avail ourselves to such. This conclusion was arrived at by someone, actually the author, who at one time strongly detested and was suspicious of reincarnation!

CHAPTER 27

Are Earthlings God's Chosen And Only People

Another interesting belief of the Christian faiths is the belief that this is the only planet which contains "humanoid" beings, or life forms. This belief, probably originating with the early Catholic Church and the concept of a geocentric earth (center of the solar system) is quite vulnerable to the recent findings of astronomy, space exploration, science, and the studies of ancient religion. For a fact, we know that that Sun is the center of our solar system.

Secondly, we have the pictures from the Mariner 9 NASA probe and pictures from the Viking 1 and 2 NASA probes of architectural remains on the planet Mars. Some of these pictures are printed in, *The Monuments of Mars,* by Richard Hoagland and in *The Keys of Enoch,* by Dr. Hurtak. Many of these remains closely replicate the Sphinx figure in Egypt and actually exceed the pyramid complexes in Egypt, China, and Mexico.

Thirdly, we have the acknowledgement from the ancient Sanskrit teachings that the origin of these teachings is extraterrestrial. Also, the Cherokee attribute the source of their teachings to be from the Pleiades constellation of stars. We also have paintings of space craft in Peruvian ancient ruins surrounding Machu Pichu. Further, we have evidence of what appears to be huge airfields in the Nasca Plain in Peru and the Mojave Desert in California, dwarfing anything we have today. These quite conceivably could have been used as spaceports.

In addition, we have architectural wonders on the earth, most notably in Egypt, China, Peru, England, and Mexico, which probably could not even be constructed by our finest architects, engineers, and construction companies today. Who built these structures and where did the knowledge for creating such buildings and structures come from, considering it would be impossible for us to replicate them today, even with our great engineering knowledge and experience.

Besides all of this, there has been such a proliferation of sightings and verifications of UFO's, even taking into account that many people were imagining things or hallucinating in regard to their sightings, there is a strong actuality that there are many other "humanoid" beings or life forms visiting our planet from other parts of the universe. This is documented in Zechariah Sitchin's books, such as *When Time Began* and *The Twelve Planet* and Robert Temple's *The Sirius Mystery*. Astronomers have recently identified and indexed over 100 billion planets and stars in just our galaxy, the Milky Way. And, there are *at least* 100 billion galaxies besides our own. This does not even include parallel Galaxies and Universes. That all of these other planets are just barren spheres is an insult to the creativity and ingenuity of our creator—GOD! As such, IT IS BEYOND UNLIKELY THAT EARLINGS ARE GOD'S CHOSEN OR ONLY PEOPLE! And if Earth was the Creator's best effort, the author would be astonished!

CHAPTER 28

Is One Earth Religion Chosen Over The Others?

With a fanaticism that terrifies many people, including the author, there are religions which claim to be the chosen belief of God to the exclusion of all other beliefs. This fanatical tenet seems to be central to Christianity and Islam (Moslem). In the case of Christianity, it is indeed true that the Bible is presented as "the word of God." Unfortunately for Christians and the same would apply to Moslems, THERE IS NO PLACE IN THE BOOKS OF EITHER OF THESE FAITHS WHICH SAYS "THEIR WORDS" ARE THE *ONLY* WORDS OF GOD!!!!.

If God created everything, Quantum Physics, Quantum Mechanics, and Quantum Arithmetic, as the various scriptures and spiritual sciences seem to strongly indicate, then God must have created all of the earth's religions likewise. Is God so prejudiced and mono-dimensional that It would create many religions and then favor one over the others? Would not it just be simpler and more economical to have created just the one "chosen" religion, excluding the creation of all others? And, is there any justice in a Hindu who never had the chance to be exposed to Christianity to be excluded from Heaven and/or condemned to Hell.

People who have the compulsion and near sightedness of vision to only think of their religion as the "chosen" one, are often likely to feel very insecure or uncertain in their chosen belief, although this may not be apparent at first glance. Thus they feel compelled to convince other people of the correctness of their belief so that they can convince themselves that their religion is the "chosen" one.

WHEN WE GET PAST THE DOGMA AND POLITICS OF THE WORLD'S RELIGIONS, WE BEGIN TO UNVEIL THE REAL ESSENCE OF THE FUNDAMENTAL BELIEFS INVOLVED. AS THIS DOGMA IS TRANSCENDED, WE FIND THAT ALL RELIGIONS ARE QUITE SIMILAR AND THEIR DIFFERENCES ARE ONLY THE RESULT OF CULTURAL INFLUENCES AND BIAS. In the Baha'i faith, the validity of all religions and all of the "masters" of these religions including Krishna, Rama, Lao-Tze, Zoroaster, Buddha, Jesus, Quetzocoatl, Mohammed, and more, are exalted, as they well should be since the creator of these religions and "masters" is God. By revering and respecting all of God's creations, including all of our religions, it is more respectful of our creator to accept the validity of all religions, rather than shunning religions contrary to one's chosen belief.

Knowing that all religions are the "word of God" allows us to have respect and tolerance for those beliefs contrary to the one we personally embrace at this time. When many people can accept this idea, most, if not all of our wars, will end as the irrational hatred between differing religions is eliminated!

CHAPTER 29

Does Satan Possess Us And Run Our Lives?

Now that we have "stirred up the waters" even more, let us examine the question of whether Satan—the Devil—can possess us and run our lives. This again is a concept which has a fundamental importance to most Christians and Moslems today. It is fervently believed that there is this extremely powerful entity that can possess us, cause us to do terrible things, and separate us from God. It certainly is evident at times that most of us do things which do not glorify the higher aspects of God. But, are we being controlled by the 'Devil' while doing these things?

While there is no Satan or Devil in the eastern religions, there is a concept somewhat akin to this. In Taoism, this is known as Yin, and is associated with negativity and darkness. A basic difference between Yin and Satan however, is that there is no ascertainment as to the "goodness" or "badness" of this "negativity". In *Science and Health with Key to the Scriptures,* Mary Baker Eddy unconditionally states that there is no place for error, Satan, or sin, in the perfection of God's creation as revealed in the First Chapter of Genesis in the Bible. Certainly we could conclude that if God fills all space, as Mary Baker Eddy so powerfully states, then the Devil or Satan, at best, is an illusion, albeit a powerful one.

One thing which we know today is that the power of thoughts which emanate from our mind is such a potent expression of electromagnetic energy, that such thoughts, when focused with intensity, can literally manifest and/or change creation, events, and things. This is discussed in Ken Keyes" book, *The Hundredth Monkey* and in Jane Robert's, *The Nature of Personal Reality.* We can measure the electrical nature of the brainwaves associated with these thoughts on an EEG machine. Also remember our earlier experience with the power of our words, which was measured in conjunction with arm muscle testing.

There are some "Masters", such as Sathya Sai Baba in India, who can materialize things from the ethers (the Electromagnetic energy field that pervades God's Creations) which did not exist in the physical world only moments before. Our thoughts are equally powerful, if not more so, in creating negative experiences. Thus when we focus our thoughts on Satan, sin, emotional trauma, fear, anger, and revenge, we will create the illusion of Satan and sin in our lives. But all of these things are not from God, and only exist in the minds of men—not God! Therefore, they can have no factual reality in the scheme of creation.

This whole Satan/sin syndrome is circumvented by concentrating our thoughts on God and such positive things such as joy, humor, laughter, and thanksgiving. As is revealed in *The Keys of Enoch,* as we allow ourselves to be conduits of the "Living Light" (God), we transcend the consciousness of sin. Thus, as we desire, strive for, and achieve glorifying our creator, Satan/sin naturally disappears from our lives.

Satan/sin is also overcome by meditation and meditation related disciplines. Such things as a sitting meditation or the Tai Chi Standing Meditation are practices which bring us closer to God, thereby bringing more balanced to our lives so that we are less prone to outbursts of anger, resentment, revenge, etc. Since God fills all space via the pervasive electromagnetic/light force field, there is in reality nothing else. We claim and create this by actively entertaining God and maintaining positive experiences in our consciousness. These things are achieved by remaining emotionally balanced. This is what everything in this book helps us to know and accomplish in our experiencing God. Thus it is our responsibility to avail ourselves to use these methods, means, devices, and practices if we are to know God more meaningfully!

Thus we could say that God does not create sickness and disease, nor are they punishments. Therefore man in reality cannot be afflicted by them, no matter how convincing the evidence or symptoms. Rather, we ourselves created our sicknesses and disease (lack of ease) through our thoughts and emotions, mainly consisting of fear, anger, resentment and depression! This is clearly stated in *Science and Health with Key to the Scriptures,* by Mrs. Eddy and Louise L. Hay in, *You Can Heal Your Life.*

But the question still remains, how does man heal himself from sickness and disease or the illusions there from? Also, can God heal us? In a real sense, neither God nor anyone else, including a highly skilled doctor can heal us of anything since sickness and disease are the results of uncontrolled lower emotional expressions just described in the previous paragraph (depression, anger, fear, and resentment). WHEN WE TAKE THESE LOWER EMOTIONS OUT OF OUR CONSCIOUSNESS, A RETURN TO HEALTH IS THE NATURAL RESULT!

Other books chronicling this emotion-sickness connection during the last few years are numerous and include among others: *Who Gets Sick,* by Blair Justice; *Your Emotions and Your Health,* by Emrika Padus, et., al.; *Mending the Body, Mending the Mind,* by Joan Borysenko; *The Healing Brain,* by Robert Ornstein and David Sobel; *The Psychobiology of Mind-Body Healing,* by Ernest Lawrence Rossi; and books by Bernie Siegel and Norman Cousins.

By correcting our emotional responses and mental outlook, we can effectuate healing. God can be very instrumental in bringing about the anchoring of the higher emotions (happiness, joy, humor, laughter) in our daily experience and thus create our normal and rightful condition—health. THESE HIGHER EMOTIONAL STATES ARE A POWERFUL ANTIDOTE AGAINST SICKNESS AND DISEASE!

So we could say that the more we are at one with God, the healthier will be our emotions, body, and mind. We, and not God or doctors, are responsible for the health of our body, mind, and emotions!

Refer to Dr. Newton's *A Map to Healing and Your Essential Divinity Through Theta Consciousness,* FOR SPECIFIC HEALING PROTOCOLS CONTAINED IN CHAPTER FOUR. There is also a discussion of emotions that can be carried our DNA from our previous lives and those of our relatives and ancestors.

CHAPTER 30

Does God Create Sickness, Disease And Death

The prevailing belief is that God/good is responsible in some way shape or form for the maladies and calamities that seem to beset us. For the author, earlier in his life, this was his belief, at least in some sense. However, he came change this view upon his exposure to Mary Baker Eddy, the founder of Christian Science. The things we experience are the reality that we create from our thoughts and emotions, be they conscious or subconscious. The "computer"/brain replicates experiences in our lives in conformance with the information to which it has been exposed to/programmed with. How to undo such misprogramming/ malprogramming is discussed in detail in Dr. Newton's, "A Map to Healing and Your Essential Divinity Through Theta Consciousness". The God that the author knows and experiences would never even wish, let alone create, anything except good and wonderful things for his creation!!!!

CHAPTER 31

Who's The Boss?

A curious synchronicity occurs over and over again in the annals of Western religions and governments. This recurring theme is the idea that men are superior to women, and that men are stronger, more intelligent, superior in logic, more creative, and better able to rule. It is claimed by Christians that the Bible, and by the Moslems that the Koran, attributes this superiority given by God to men and not women. In the teachings of the Old Testament of the Bible, there is probably no doubt of the asserted superiority of men, or the perceived superiority!

However, the "kinder, gentler" New Testament cannot realistically support such an assertion. Looked at objectively by scientific studies which we have today, in reality, and in general, we can only say that men are superior to women in muscle strength, and the gap in this category is getting smaller. In other "strengths" such as health and longevity of life, women are clearly stronger than men!

Furthermore, we know that the brainwaves of women are the same as those of men, that women have the same brain hemispheres of about the same size, and that women can be and are at least as intelligent, logical, and creative as men! So, where does this purportedly God given concept of the superiority of men come from, God or man? Judged by the scientific data we have today and taking away the Jewish cultural prejudices (namely the inferiority of women) at the time the Old Testament was written, we could logically conclude that such concepts were created by men. Obviously, and not surprisingly, RELIGION HAS BEEN USED TO SUBJUGATE AND CONTROL WOMEN!

In her book, *When God Was a Woman,* Merlin Stone has detailed not only the processes and means by which men established control over women, but actually how women may very likely have been considered superior to and ruled men, in times past. Among a Christian sect, the Gnostics, the power of women is acknowledged and revered. In the native American traditions and religion, women also are revered. The Cherokee Indians have two laws: the first law is, "Do nothing to hurt the children"; the second law is, "Everything is born of woman".

In Taoism is the concept of Yin (feminine) and Yang (masculine). And both of these concepts are of equal importance. If one becomes more important than the other, the forces of creation and harmony become unbalanced and the earth experiences unproductive extremes in religion, government, business, and family life. In the first chapter of Genesis in the Bible, we have the clear words that: "So God created man in his own image, in the image of God created He him; male and female created He them."

This is the clearest indication here that male and female were created on an equal basis. Nothing is even implied about the inferiority of women until the Garden of Eden and this could have been nothing more than a description of extraterrestrial peoples who displeased their ruler, as per the descriptions in the various Zecharia Sitchin books.

Often, people who themselves feel inferior, have this subconscious compulsion to control, dominate, and belittle those people who are actually "better" than themselves. Possibly this is why women became subjugated to men. But it is highly unlikely that such an inferior status was given to women by God. This was the creation of the Jewish, Catholic, Protestant and Islamic religions. Instead of men focusing on "bossing" women, they might be wiser to invest their energy and thoughts to recognizing the real boss in this Universe—God

CHAPTER 32

Does True Happiness Come From Intimate Relationships Or God?

While it appears that there has been a crusade against Christians and Christianity in this book, there is no intention to denigrate the teachings of Christ viewed from the highest spiritual intent. As Christianity has matured and "aged", there has been a gradual dilution of the "high spiritual intent". THINGS THAT ARE DONE BY CHRISTIANS IN THE NAME OF JESUS, WHICH HE WOULD NOT HAVE DONE HIMSELF OR CONDONED, WOULD REPULSE THE "GREAT MASTER"!

However, in the area of relationship priority, the purity of Christianity has remained intact. This is because the Christian faiths teach that a person's most intimate relationship, first and foremost, is with God. This is in stark contradiction to much of humanity which has over-romanticized and mis-prioritized the importance of not only romantic, but also friendship and familial relationships. The painfully obvious result of this is that despite more material wealth, comforts, and activities than any other time in recent history, many Americans and Europeans are very unhappy and disillusioned. This is so even in light of most people having some type of romantic relationship and many friends!

Obviously today in romantic relationships there is widespread unhappiness and disappointment along with a spiraling divorce rate and other relationship disasters. Even as people may have a satisfying romantic relationship with another person, too frequently romantic happiness is a fleeting phenomenon. Why? Because our priority in romantic relationships is askew! As we become romantically involved with someone in the beginning, a happiness and relaxation occurs which results in many endorphins being released into the body and we feel great! Also because we are relaxed, more of God's electromagnetic energy courses throughout our bodies creating an even greater ecstasy!

In such a condition, we are so swept up in the feelings and events of the romantic entanglement, we lose perspective of the event and make a number of incorrect conclusions. Not only for the author, but in the lives of people he has known, we begin to attribute these wonderful things in our lives to our romantic partner. In a blindness that later comes back to haunt us, we attribute qualities of perfection to our partners which they do not in reality express at that time. In our minds we envision this person as the most wonderful being in the world even though in reality they may fall far short of this. This is not because our partner is not a Divine creation of our Creator but rather they have been programmed to believe they are anything but Divine!

In essence, we attribute these wonderful things happening in our lives to our partner. In reality, such "wonderfulness" has less to do with our loved one and more to do with a strong presence of God which has expressed itself in our lives. By not giving the credit to the source of our happiness, God, this initially wonderful situation can become more disastrous than wonderful. And this is essentially true because we do not give thanks and acknowledgment to God for these wonderful feelings.

Christians stress the importance of putting God first in our lives before all other things, including romantic relationships. This is imperative along with the concept of realizing that all good things that happen to us are created by God! With this perspective, our lives will be more enjoyable and fruitful. Furthermore, the lack of dependability of our fellow man is so certain, that God is the only thing which we can truly depend on to always be there for us in a time of need. True happiness then, comes from God—not romance! Romance is nice, in fact great, but our relationship with God is essential to our real happiness and success. Without this understanding, disaster usually shortly occurs in our romantic lives!

CHAPTER 33

Is Science An Insult To God?

Many people in fundamentalist religions or beliefs feel that science has no place in religion or should even be taught at all. It is claimed by these fundamentalists that such science is the "word of the devil". Unfortunately this is an easy, although inaccurate depiction of something which conflicts with and disproves our current religious beliefs. The problem for many centuries, religious beliefs were basically unchallenged by any empirical evidence. Now, many things can be empirically photographed, observed, and measured by instruments and can be charted—things that would not have been dreamed possible, even several decades ago. Thus, science is and will continue to redefine and to refine religious concepts and understanding. And that is good for humanity at large since as was stated in the *Gospel of Thomas,* BELIEF WITHOUT UNDERSTANDING IS OF LITTLE VALUE!

Part of the scientific problem stems from Darwin's theory of evolution, which began a religious furor in the middle 1800's to the present. Darwin claimed to have arrived at his conclusions by scientific observations. Unfortunately, Darwin's powers of observation were probably quite clouded at times, and thus his proposals are not scientifically provable, but rather personally held beliefs and theories. Science, with its wonderful new instruments, is able to begin to measure and quantify the presence of God. This would include electromagnetism, light, color, vibration, motion, and sound so often referred to in this book. Unfortunately for those with dogmatic or closed views of God, WHILE SCIENCE IS BEGINNING TO PROVE THE EXISTENCE OF GOD, AT THE SAME TIME SCIENCE IS INVALIDATING DOGMATIC, BLIND BELIEFS AND IDEAS which have been "cherished" for hundreds and thousands of years!

Thus, we can conclude that science is beneficial to God but not to status quo religions, who refuse to re-examine their beliefs in light of new evidence. This is clearly revealed in such books as *The Keys of Enoch,* by Dr. J. J. Hurtak, and *Stalking the Wild Pendulum* and *The Cosmic Book,* by Itzhak Benton. These books are examples of individuals searching for and finding the convergence and cross verification between science and the ancient spiritual traditions. As science advances in its knowledge and ability to measure heretofore undetectable phenomenon, the trend of science to prove the existence of God will become even more preponderant and established religions may protest against this even louder as their "cherished" beliefs fade away!

CHAPTER 34

Aligning And Surrendering Ourselves To God In Our Daily Thoughts And Actions

T O KNOW GOD BETTER WE MUST HAVE THE CONSCIOUS AND SUBCONSCIOUS DESIRE TO DO SO! Once we have this state of mind, THERE WILL BE THE REQUISITE PERSERVERANCE to see us through the completion of our tasks to the next level. We have the INNATE ABILITY TO ALIGN OURSELVES WITH AND SURRENDER TO GOD, in our thoughts and actions at all times. However, since we have been given "free will",—the distinct ability to choose a path other than that which glorifies God—we often stray from the pathway which leads us to God. This "straying" effect is most often attributed to the Devil/ Satan. However, this is actually the result of our being depressed, fearful, angry, and resentful in regard to people, places, and things! These emotions, as has been mentioned many times previously in this book, act to prevent or block us from experiencing our God on a continual basis.

In order to counteract these non-productive emotions of depression, anger, fear, and resentment, it takes a continual concentrated effort to focus on the "positive" things occurring in our lives. Admittedly, this is a difficult process when we are surrounded by turmoil at home or at work or wherever. But if we are TO TRANSCEND THE ILLUSION OF TURMOIL, INEQUITY, ETC., WE MUST FORCE OURSELVES TO SEE AND ACKNOWLEDGE THE PERFECTION OF GOD'S CREATION, which is everything and the only thing!.

By emphasizing the higher emotions of happiness, joy, humor and laughter, instead of the lower emotions previously mentioned such as fear, anger, resentment and depression, we are able to concentrate on knowing the perfection of the universe and the perfection of the human species created in the image and likeness of God. THIS IS BECAUSE THE HIGHER EMOTIONS OF HAPPINESS, ETC NATURALLY ALIGN US WITH GOD'S PRESENCE AND GUIDANCE. As such, we are more likely to concentrate on everything which is positive in our lives. This is programmed and reinforced into our minds by being grateful for every positive thing which happens in our life—no matter how small or insignificant. These concepts are discussed in Arnold M. Patnet's book, *You Can Have It All, Treat Yourself to Life,* by Raymond Charles Barker, and in great depth in *Science and Health With Key to the Scriptures,* by Mary Baker Eddy.

The obvious question which must be asked is, how is this accomplished? One answer is that WE MUST CONTROL AND REPROGRAM THE HUMAN MIND-COMPUTER, AS WELL AS THE SUBCONSCIOUS MIND, through the use of affirmations, subliminal tapes, or Neurolinguistic programming. If these methods are used in the prescribed manner outlined in earlier chapters in this book, our thoughts will gradually begin to turn more to God and we then can experience God's caring for us.

Mary Baker Eddy emphasizes that we must protect ourselves from "aggressive mental suggestion" (all sorts of negative thoughts) on an hourly and daily basis. Only by such a persistent effort, can we know and experience God more profoundly in our lives. The more we strive to acknowledge and see the actual perfection of the universe and all of its by products, the more this becomes literally apparent in our lives. This gives us a clear indication that we are becoming "closer" to God. According to Arnold Patent, this acknowledgment of universal perfection becomes easier and is facilitated by our ability to transcend logical, rational thought patterns which block and hide God's presence from us. In other words, WE MUST BREAK AWAY FROM OUR EXISTING PATTERNS OF THOUGHT AND HABITS TO MORE FULLY EXPERIENCE GOD! Usually, this will not usually happen overnight, but rather as a gradual and ongoing process. At times it may even seem that we regress in our efforts to perceive and affirm the perfection of God's creation. But, as we are persistent in our efforts to do so, it will be manifested in our lives!

IN CHAPTER FOUR OF DR. NEWTON'S BOOK, *A Map to Healing and Your Essential Divinity,* ARE REPROGRAMMING PROTOCOLS FOR CHANGING OUR PATTERNS OF THOUGHTS, EMOTIONS, AND HABITS. This is "leading edge" mind programming technology involving "Theta Consciousness Healing"! This can also be programmed using Neurolinguistic Programming discussed in Chapter Four of this book.

CHAPTER 35

How To Reap God's Abundance For Our Lives

Much of the information from this chapter comes from *You Can Have It All,* by Arnold Patent, *Treat Yourself to Life,* by Raymond Charles Barker, and *Science and Health With Key to the Scriptures,* by Mary Baker Eddy. A complete reading of these books is highly recommended. to create abundance in your life, which includes more than just money, a nice car, and a big home! TO CHANGE THINGS IN YOUR LIFE, IT IS NECESSARY TO ACCEPT THE SITUATION YOU ARE IN AT THIS TIME—EVEN IF YOU ARE IN DEBT!!!!

And then you must recognize that ANY SHORTAGE OF MONEY (or anything else) IS JUST AN *ILLUSION!* To help in transcending the illusion of lack, we need to feel good about paying off our creditors. Realize any shortages we experience are our resistance to God's abundance for us. Then recognize that the creation of debt is not a bad thing you have done, and there is nothing wrong with your creditor wanting to be repaid.

Now you are ready to choose and visualize the abundance that you now want to manifest and experience, thus see this as if it were already true at this time. There is a divergence of thought on the next step.

Some people feel that you turn the whole matter over to God and let God handle the details since God can do this better than we can. Other people feel that you must focus with great detail or details on what you want to manifest. Personally, the author has had results both ways so you must use your own intuition in deciding which way is right for you.

Finally, it is important that we see and feel ourselves being abundant as much as possible throughout the day. BE AWARE OF ANY AND ALL SIGNS OF ABUNDANCE IN YOUR LIFE, no matter how small. GIVE **THANKS** FOR THIS ABUNDANCE! This is especially critical since we have been programmed since our days as young children that there are limited resources and wealth which we can possess. AS YOU GIVE THANKS FOR **GOD'S UNLIMITED ABUNDANCE**, YOU ARE PRIMING THE PUMP TO RECEIVE MORE PROPSERITY AND MANIFESTATION IN YOUR LIFE and counteracting the constant play back from the subconscious mind that we are lacking or can lack something in our lives.

Intellectual decisions will not bring abundance and prosperity into your life, but **FOCUSED DESIRE AND PERSERVERANCE WILL**. If you are still having problems believing that you really can be abundant and prosperous, consider that everything on our planet and cosmos can be reduced to energy—much of it being the electromagnetic energy we have discussed so thoroughly in this book. And we further know that this energy and its source, most likely God, is extremely pervasive and prolific.

Thus, **SINCE MONEY AND OTHER FORMS OF ABUNDANCE ARE LIKEWISE ENERGY, THERE IS CERTAINLY ENOUGH ENERGY ABUNDANCE FOR ALL OF US TO BE PROSPEROUS!** While we may not be able to create money/abundance in our lives instantly, or even in a month, we can still do so over a period of time if we apply the concepts and ideas presented in this chapter. One major hurdle or delay to us manifesting such a **SUBCONSCIOUS BELIEF THAT WE ARE NOT WORTHY OF ACCUMULATING WEALTH,** or even that wealth is either 'evil' or 'bad'. In none of the spiritual traditions has the author been able to find verification that wealth is evil or bad. However, man's, not God's, interpretation of these traditions has cast a negative connotation on the accumulation of wealth.

One powerful way to counteract this limiting and distorted perception is to consider that our **MANIFESTING ABUNDANCE IS PROOF OF OUR ALIGNMENT AND UNDERSTANDING OF GOD AND GOD'S ACTUAL EXPRESSION IN OUR LIVES**!

Abundance can be programmed into our subconscious–computer using the Neurolinguistic Programming technique of "swishing", discussed in Chapter Four of this book. This can also be powerfully accomplished using the "Theta Consciousness Healing" protocol in Chapter Four of Dr. Newton's, *A Map to Healing and Your Essential Divinity Through Theta Consciousness*!

CHAPTER 36

The Still Small Voice Within

As has been expressed by every religious tradition, we have a God on which we can rely for guidance and inspiration. There have been many ways described in this book in which we can more profoundly contact and experience the presence of God. What must be remembered, as Mark Thurson points out in *Experiments in a Search for God, is* that you cannot force God into your life. Also, expectations seem to thwart experiencing the presence of God. Instead of trying very hard to find God, it will happen naturally if we just let it be known that we want it and take steps which allow it to occur!

What are those steps? **THEY ARE A STRONG AND CONTINUOUS DESIRE, DEDICATING OURSELVES TO KNOWING AND MIRRORING GOD MORE FULLY IN OUR DAILY LIVES!**

Know also that the methods, devices, and means in finding God are tools. **DO NOT CONFUSE "TOOLS" TO KNOWING GOD AS BEING GOD—THEY JUST ALLOW GREATER ACCESS TO GOD**. To link with God, become very still or relaxed and use full diaphragmatic breathing. Continue to advance your relaxation so far that you begin to lose consciousness in, or concern about, your body.

Then be aware of mental impressions for guidance and inspiration from God.

Remember that these impressions are usually subtle or fleeting, and usually are not repeated on the same day. **MANY TIMES, PEOPLE FIND THAT THEIR PRAYERS AND MEDITATIONS ARE ENHANCED THROUGH FIRST INVOKING THE HELP OF ACKNOWLEDGED MASTERS** such as Jesus, Buddha, Kuthumi, Krishna, Asclepius, Michael (A.K.A Helios, Apollo), Hermes, Thoth, Enoch, Ra, Misol Ha) and others. The presence of these masters in service to God, can be invoked through mantras, visualization, or pictures of the masters.

WITH GOD ON/AT OUR SIDE, WE CAN SURVIVE ANYTHING, AND EVEN THRIVE IN THE MOST DIFFICULT SITUATIONS. Many great spiritual teachers have said over the ages, that one person with God constitutes a majority. My wish then, is that you be blessed enough to be in that majority!!!

Bibliography

A New Encyclopedia of Freemasonry, by Arthur Edward White, Weathervane Books, N.Y. *A Search for God,* A.R.E. Press, VA Beach, VA.

Apollonius of Tyana, by G.S.R. Mead, Ares Publishers, Inc., Chicago, IL.

Asklepios: The Cult of the Greek God of Medicine, by Alice Walton, Ares Publishers Inc., Chicago, IL.

Back to Eden, by Jethro Kloss, Back to Eden Books, Loma Linda, CA.

Choose Once Again: Selections from A Course in Miracles, by Foundation for Inner Peace, Celestial Arts, CA

Color and the Edgar Cayce Readings, by Roger Lewis, A.R.E. Press, VA Beach, VA.

Cosmic Crystals: Crystal Consciousness and the New Age, by Ra Bonewitz, Turnstone Press Ltd., Welling borough, Northampton shire, England.

Crystal Enlightenment & Crystal Healing, by Katrina Raphaell, Aurora Press, NY.Y., N.Y. *Earth Changes Update,* by Hugh Lynn Cayce, A.R.E. Press, Virginia Beach, VA

Experiments in a Search for God, by Mark A Thurson, A.R.E. Press, VA Beach, VA.

Folk Medicine: The Art and Science, edited by Richard P. Steiner, American Chemical Society, Washington, DC

Gems and Stones, A.R.E. Press, VA Beach, VA

Gems, Stones, and Metals, by Carol Baraff, Heritage Publications

Harmonies and Tones and Colors, by Hughes

Have You Heard the Great Pyramid Speaks, Mikkel Dahl, Sheperdsfield, Falton, MO.

Inventions, Researches and Writings of Nikola Tesla, by Thomas Commerford Martin, Angriff Press, Hollywood, CA.

Kundalini for the New Age, Gopi Krishna, Bantam Books, N.Y.

Life Force, Leo F. Ludzia, Llewellyn Publications, St. Paul, MM

Negative Ions, Kurt W. Donsbach & Morton Walker, Wholistic Publications, Rosarito Beach, Baja Calif., Mexico.

New Frontiers, a magazine of transformation published by The New Frontier Educational Society. (Especially valuable is the December, 1989 issue.), 46 N. Front Street, Philadelphia, PA 19106

Nourishing the Life Force, Richard and Mary-Alice Jafolla, Unity Books, Unity Village, MO.

Pole Shift, John White, A.R.E. Press, VA Beach, VA

Pyramid Power & Beyond Pyramid Power, by G. Patrick Flanagan, De Vorss & Co., Marina del Rey, CA

Radionics Interface with the Ether Fields, by Dr. David V. Tansley, C.W. Daniel Co., Ltd., Saffron Walden, England.

Reincarnation: The Phoenix Fire Mystery, Joseph Head and S.L. Cranston, Julian Atlantic Press/Crown Publishers, Inc., N.Y., N.Y.

Science and Health with Key to the Scriptures, by Mary Baker Eddy, Christian Science Publishing Society, Boston, MA. (Available at any Christian Science Reading Room)

Scientific Basis and Build of Music, by Ramsay

Scientific Healing Affirmations, by Paramahansa Yogananda, Self Realization Fellowship, L.A., CA.

Secrets of the Soil, by Peter Tompkins

Seeds of Wisdom, Vol. 2, by Pundit Ravi Shankar

Simple Things and Simple Thoughts, by Dr. Eldon Taylor, Just Another Reality, Box 7116, Salt Lake City, UT.

Sound Medicine, Leah Maggie Garfield, Celestial Arts, Berkeley, CA

Stalking the Wild Pendulum & The Cosmic Book, by Itzhak Bentov, Bantam Books, N.Y.

Subliminal Communication, by Dr. Eldon Taylor, Just Another Reality, Box 7116, Salt Lake City, UT 84107.

Subliminal Learning: An Eclectic Approach Force, by Dr. Eldon Taylor, Just Another Reality, Box 7116, Sal Lake City, UT 84107.

Sympathetic Vibratory Physics, a journal by Delta Spectrum Research, 1309 Chestnut, Colorado Springs, CO 80905

Taking the Quantum Leap, by Fred an Wolf, Harper and Row, San Francisco, CA *The Aquarian Gospel of Jesus the Christ,* by Levi, De Vorss & Co., Publishers

The Body Electric: Electromagnetism and the Foundation of Life, Dr. Robert Becker, William Morrow and Co., Inc., N.Y. N.Y.

The Book of the Secrets, by Bhagwan Shree Rajneesh (now called Osho), Harper and Row,

The Bridge to Infinity, by Bruce L. Cathie, America West Publishers. P.O. Box K, Boulder, CO 80306

The Chromium Program, by Dr. Jeffrey A. Fisher

The Crown of Life, by Kirpal Singh, Divine Science of the Soul, Ruhani, Satsang, India.

The Crystal Book & Crystal Healing Book, by Dael Walker, The Crystal Company, Books, *Pacheco, CA.*

The Death of Ignorance, Dr. Frederick Bell, (out of print; Possibly available from Paradyne, Inc. 891 Santa Ana, Laguna Beach, CA 92651).

The Gospel of the Essenes, by Edmond Bordeaux Szekely, The C.W. Daniel Co. Ltd., Saffron Waldon, England

The Holy Bible

The Keys of Enoch, Dr. J.J. Hurtak, The Academy for Future Science, Los Gatos, CA. *The Lost Books of the Bible,* Bell Publishing Co., N.Y., N.Y.

The Monuments of Mars: A City on the Edge of Forever, Richard C. Hoagland, North Atlantic Books, Berkeley, CA.

The Mystical Qabalah, by Dion Fortune, Samuel Weiser, Inc., York Beach, ME.

The Pleasure Connection, by Deva and James Beck, Synthesis Press, San Marcos, CA. *The Rosey Tablet,* by Gandolph Slick, The Renaissance Foundation, Ft. Wayne, IN. *The Secret Life of Plants,* by Peter Tompkins

The Secret Teachings of All Ages, Manly P. Hall, Philosophical Research Society, Inc., L.A., CA 90027.

The Spiritual Value of Gemstones, by Wally Richardson & Lenora Huett, De Vorss & Co. Marina del Rey, CA

Toning: The Creative Power of the Voice, by Laurel Elizabeth Keyes, De Vorss & Co., Marina del Rey, CA.

Treat Yourself to Life, by Raymond Charles Barker, Dodd, Mead, and Co., N.Y.

Treat Yourself, by Dr. Jack Prince, Possibly available from Burdett Enterprises, P.O. Box 538, Santa Rosa, CA 95402

Your Emotions and Your Health, by Emrika Padus, Rodale Press, Emmaus, PA.